THE JIGSAW PUZZLE OF LIFE

CLEAR ANSWERS TO COMPLICATED PROBLEMS

JOE JORDAN

Order this book online at www.trafford.com
or email orders@trafford.com

Most Trafford titles are also available at major online book retailers.

Scripture quotations marked KJV are from the Holy Bible, King James Version
(Authorized Version). First published in 1611. Quoted from the KJV Classic
Reference Bible, Copyright © 1983 by The Zondervan Corporation.

Print information available on the last page.

ISBN: 978-1-4907-9705-2 (sc)
ISBN: 978-1-4907-9707-6 (hc)
ISBN: 978-1-4907-9706-9 (e)

Library of Congress Control Number: 2019913149

Trafford rev. 09/04/2019

www.trafford.com
North America & international
toll-free: 1 888 232 4444 (USA & Canada)
fax: 812 355 4082

This book is dedicated to my sweet wife, Melva.

She has always been my greatest source of encouragement in every moment of our earthly sojourn.

I also want to express my deep gratitude to my sister and brothers-in-law, Barbara and Jerry Teboe for their help and encouragement

Foreword

(Paige Patterson)

Fishing on a beautiful lake in the Alaskan wilderness, I found it difficult to concentrate. The image of towering Mount McKinley was overpowering. My young guide Seth said, "If you intend to catch any fish, you must concentrate and do what I tell you." Here was a youth instructing a man seventy-seven years old on how to do something I have done all my life. And everything Seth told me was exactly right. Knowing a given lake, familiar with the fish, conversant with the bait, sporting expertise in methodology, Seth taught the older angler how to have success. Doing things as Seth directed proved true and I caught fish.

Joe Jordan, author of *The Jigsaw Puzzle of Life,* has spent his lifetime teaching young people how to put the puzzle of their lives into perspective with a view to completing beautiful artistry. Creating *Word of Life* camps around the world, at first under the direction of Jack Wyrtzen and later as the leader of *Word of Life International,* Jordan blazed a prophetic trail going where few saints of God have ever ventured. Following principles vividly articulated by Jordan, multitudes of youth have made the transition from "rags to riches," not in terms of acquiring perishing wealth but in terms of attaining eternal prosperity.

The book you hold in your hand is a distillation of the thinking and teaching of Joe Jordan, a man used of God to transform the lives of an army of young people and to create aggressive mission vistas throughout the world. I remember visiting *Word of Life – Argentina* for the first time. I could never decide what astonished me most. Where did all of these bright kids come from? What brought them there to study? How did they learn so much in so few years? And why were their hearts so compassionate? These young women and men were not parrots trained to repeat a few lines taught by Jordan. Having adopted the principles expounded in this book, they had become able theologians and Bible students on their own. That is why I am grateful that Jordan took the time to write this volume.

Jordan combines the knowledge of a theologian with the insights of a gifted preacher, the vision of a missionary, the experience of a biblical counselor, and the intensity of an evangelist to provide a perspective as unique as it is biblical. Beginning with the evidences for the existence of a personal God and moving to the purposes of God, Jordan challenges young women and men in their basic thinking. Chapter following chapter reveals biblical answers and assessments of how to counter temptation without becoming a victim and how to engage in healthy evangelism in such a manner that others come to know Christ. How does someone select a healthy regimen of music? Are there biblical principles that will assist in finding a life's mate? And what does biblical prophecy have to do with life's meaning? These are just a few of the questions with cogent answers provided in this classic presentation.

Did I mention youth? Yes – but this volume has a broader purpose. What about those who minister to young people? Or, it is the case that you are a parent attempting to stake out some approach that has a modicum of chance to present gifted and committed youth to a desperate world? I remain convinced that any thoughtful person will profit immensely from *The Jigsaw Puzzle of Life*. But the lasting and most promising effect of this book will be its impact on parents and youth ministers! If you are searching for a way to entertain kids long enough to get them to adulthood, and you have no more noble desire, don't waste your time with this book.

But, if your desire is to make the formative years into something more than a field of marijuana, then read this book, put these principles to work, and watch as your wonderful children become a rich field of golden wheat producing bread for themselves and others also. And while you are at it, pause and thank God that He not only placed the young in Jordan's heart but also that He led him to write for us this insight into the principles that God has used to provide blessings throughout the ages.

Paige Patterson, President
Sandy Creek Foundation
Dallas, Texas

Contents

Introduction

Have you ever tried to put together a jigsaw puzzle?

I have, but to tell you the truth, if it was very complicated, I got frustrated and quit. What I forgot to do was to maintain my focus on the picture that was on the box top of the puzzle.

It is sad to observe that is what a lot of people do with the jigsaw puzzle of life. This is especially true when they can't find clear answers to three vital questions about life: Where did I come from? Why am I here? Where am I going?

James M. Gray, who succeeded R. A. Torrey as president of Moody Bible Institute, the school founded by the world-famous evangelist D. L. Moody, said, "Who could mind the journey when the road leads home?" Yes, life is a journey but a puzzle for those who do not know where home is and how to get there.

These are three questions that almost every human asks at some point in life. Many puzzle over the implications of various potential answers before giving up and deciding to keep on living just for the moment—not concerned with any cosmic purpose or destiny.

Others tarry longer and ask another question: "Why is there something in the universe instead of nothing?"

Practically all religions and philosophies of life seek to answer these questions, with varying degrees of success for the followers of those points of view.

Since the 1990s, militant atheism has mounted an attack on organized religion, particularly Christian theism. (It would appear that it is too dangerous to attack Islamic theism!) Most recently, in the Christmas season, such atheists proudly paid for billboards that announced, "You know it's a myth. This season celebrates reason," emblazoned over a traditional picture of the magi coming to worship the Christ child.

The absurdity of such an attack underscores the pettiness of such thinkers. (1) They have no way of knowing what the reader "knows." (2) They have not even attempted to demonstrate that belief in God incarnate is unreasonable. (3) They have provided no justification for such a mean-spirited advertisement. All of which will probably result in no "conversions" from theism to atheism from this Christmas season advertisement.

Dr. Stephen Hawking, Lucasian Professor of Mathematics at Cambridge University, is considered to be the Albert Einstein of the current generation. While not mean-spirited in his critique of organized religion, his most recent book announces that there is no need for a creator God. The nature of the laws of gravity in his understanding of the theory of relativity and also quantum mechanics allows for the spontaneous generation of new universes from seemingly nothing. His famous statement from an earlier book proclaimed, "There is a singularity in our past." This "singularity" contained all the matter, energy, space, and time of our present universe in a vanishing small space of infinite density and yet spontaneously expanded in what others refer to as the big bang. Dr. Hawking claims that his mathematics demonstrate that no prime mover was necessary for this to happen in the past and that it will happen again, an infinite number of times, in the future.

It is obvious from our academic institutions and media that this "a-theist" ("no god") view of "Why am I here?" is very attractive. It negates any concern for "Where did I come from?" and makes "Where am I going?" an unimportant question with the inescapable exception that almost every rational creature is saddened to think that there will be a time in the future when we no longer exist or think.

So has this lofty pinnacle of mathematical discovery solved mankind's troubles? Has atheism, in all its forms, stopped warfare, murders, rapes? In various public forums, do practicing or practical atheists stand to testify how their convictions have improved their marriages, enriched their relationships with family and friends, brought peace and joy to their existence? In short, as a philosophy of life, does atheism help or harm mankind?

Philosophers have tried through the ages to answer these esoteric questions about the meaning of life—the puzzle of life. But here, I want to share with you how I personally found the answer to these questions and put together the puzzle of life.

My name is Joe. Not Joseph, just Joe. I was just an ordinary typical American teenager of the twentieth century as you can get. I attended a large public high school and was surrounded by the "now generation." My only passion in life was sports and to find some way to escape from a bad home situation. I had a family that was torn by anger, passion, and strife, fueled by the misuse of alcohol and scented with tobacco. I had no idea where I came from, why I was here, or where I was going. Besides whatever I could do to make myself happy, the only other motivator in life was to protect my mom and sister from my dad.

I was not hunting for any god. I suspected that one might exist but had no indication that his existence had any vital connection to mine. All this changed, however, when a WWII vet and successful businessman, Don R. Kelso, took interest in me. He wasn't after my money—I had none. He wasn't looking for a son—he had several and loved them dearly. He wasn't planning to use me as cheap labor—I had no skills or apparent talents to exploit. Looking back, there was only one human explanation for his interest in me. It was the fact that a man once took an interest in him, and that changed his life, his destination, and his destiny. With that human experience, he followed the example of Jim Welch, a local judge, and reached out to others, including me.

There was more than human involvement in this story as I have come to be convinced, as was my spiritual father and the man who won him to Christ were key in my spiritual pilgrimage. In fact, I am convinced that if we had the ability to examine the lives of those who went before, we would find an unbroken chain of compassionate servants of God all the way back to the first century when my story really began. For you see, the superhuman motivation in this story was the deep conviction that there is a God who has provided the answers to life's great questions, including the fourth one: "Why is there something in the universe instead of nothing?"

But let me tell you, as a result of God's sovereign grace, placing Don Kelso and Jack Wyrtzen in my life, how I started to put together the pieces of the jigsaw puzzle of life. It was marvelous to see how the immutable truth of Holy Scripture became the key to open the door of understanding and discernment.

Chapter One

Knowing God: Is It Reasonable to Think That He Actually Exists?

A skeptic might think that my new commitment to the absolute truth of the Word of God as a psychological response to a father figure. My own father was an alcoholic who created an abysmal home life. When a successful, respectable father figure came into my life, they would say I jumped for a chance at normalcy, love, and acceptance.

No doubt, this could be true in thousands of similar human interactions. It was true that I did respond to my spiritual father in the faith, but that does not mean there was no other force at work in the situation. Even if this is how I got on the road to this wonderful new life in Christ, it is not what has kept me in the road for over fifty years now. Why do you ask? Simply stated, it was because of him and Jack Wyrtzen I caught a passion to know more of God, which birthed within me an insatiable hunger for God's Word as the only source for faith and life.

We humans are a strange lot when it comes to logic. We act as though many things that we take for granted have been conclusively "proven" and, in our vanity, feel that most of the things we stake our lives on have been or shortly will be proven. Take simple math for instance. At first blush, does anyone question that one plus one is two? It is so easy to demonstrate with two fingers or two objects. It doesn't have to be "proven." However, think of all your friends and acquaintances. How many unbelieving friends do you have who would gladly argue, just for the sake of arguing, that one plus one does not necessarily make two but could be viewed as making "eleven"?

Nothing is "proven" merely when thinking humans are involved. In fact, both laws of physics and our legal system seek only "beyond reasonable doubt" and not necessarily "proof." We don't understand how light can be both particles and waves or created by electricity, but that doesn't stop us from flipping the light switch on. That a murderer owns the caliber of gun that killed the neighbor, had recently argued with him, is in possession of items taken from his house, and has gun powder residue on his hands does not prove that he killed the man. But motivation, means, opportunity, evidence, and proximity are enough probable cause for conviction in a court of law.

How then do humans process any truth claim? Unconsciously, we all accept the concept of unproven presuppositions as starting points, with the qualification that when pressed and challenged on the presupposition, we agree that we temporarily accept the truth claim while evaluating whether indeed it is worthy of the identification of "truth."

Despite or perhaps even with the encouragement of my admiration for my spiritual father, I accepted the presupposition that (1) there is a God, (2) He is knowable, (3) He has communicated with mankind, and (4) He has provided a way of salvation for rebellious mankind. None of these have to be immediately apparent but, once accepted, can be methodically tested against all data to the contrary.

Pilate's question "What is truth?" is answered as we rely on the God of truth, the Spirit of truth, and the Word of truth. Truth is immutable and true whether men believe it or not. Here I am after fifty years of studying God's Word, seeking His answers to this jigsaw puzzle of life, and as "the Bereans" searching the Scriptures daily, whether these things are so. As I do carry out this search, I am testifying that these four original presuppositions still ring true in my life and experiences.

Let me share with you these infallible truths, just as Dr. Luke mentioned in Acts 1:3, referring to the resurrection of Christ; he called them irrefutable, undeniable, and tangible truths.

There Is a God

Several lines of investigation continue to return a "true" to my mind.

I look at happenings in human history and realize that there is always a cause for every effect. I then ask, "What caused the universe that I see and experience?" Through the ages, atheistic skeptics have scoffingly asked, "What caused God then?" But even this cannot deter the conviction in my mind that there can be a starting point back of which we cannot go and have no need to go. In fact, that is exactly what we mean by "God"—an "Uncaused Causer." If a skeptic tries to deny the possibility of an "Uncaused Causer," he is making the same illogical mistake as the smart aleck who thinks, "Can God make a rock so big that He can't lift it?" It is not a valid question because the question pits the object against itself. By definition, it is unanswerable (another way of saying "illogical"). It is the equivalent of asking "What is the sound of yellow?" or "Draw me a triangular circle." I no more should reject the existence of God because I don't understand how electrons can make particles of light that reach my eyes at 186,000 miles per second!

I look at all the motivational drives I have experienced as a human and those that poets and songwriters and novelists and historians have chronicled and celebrated. I am thirsty, and there is liquid to drink. I am hungry, and there is food to eat. I am lonely, and there are other people similar to myself with whom to talk. I am restless, and there are places to go and things to do with my leg and arm muscles. I delight in shapes and colors, and there are myriads of objects to view and enjoy. I want to build, and there is building material with which to build. Every conceivable urge has a fulfillment in our experience. How then could we possibly conclude that the vast majority of humans in history who have sought a higher being to worship were following an urge that had no satisfaction?

I look at myself and compare myself to all other life-forms. Humans are the only earthly life-form with the ability of complex language that can be used not just for a concrete "me want grape" but also "me love the texture, color, taste, farming techniques, family memories associated with grape eating" and "I'll sell you my two grapes today for the promise of four of your grapes next fall." Where did that come from? By now, in my thinking, it is safe to assume "from the Creator God," which leads to the next logical thought "He must also be the Communicator God," and if so, does anything around here look like it has been communicated to us by Him?

Now you say, "Whoa, you're assuming what is to be proved! You know there is a book claiming to be a communication from God, and now you are pretending that you logically deduced its existence." That's right. That's how all presuppositions work. We assume it to be the case until it can be proven otherwise. I take my cue from great men of God who have been reference points in my life and the statements from the

Bible itself that there is a communicator God and that the Bible is His communication. Now I will follow up with intensive evaluation of that truth claim. The Bible claims to be the Word of God. Does it contain error? Is it illogical? Does it fall short in any way that would force me to conclude that it is less than a communication from a being we define as God? Fifty years into the evaluation, my answer is "no." It impresses me as the communication of a supreme intelligence of the classification "God."

"Why is that?" you say. Let me suggest two lines of reasoning: First, what piece of human literature was the first to be printed on the moveable-type printing press? What has been in publication continuously since the invention of the moveable-type printing press? What has been translated into more languages and copied into more copies than any other piece of literature in all human history? What book has been written over a period of 1,500 years by over forty authors writing in three languages but has no insurmountable, unexplainable, apparent contradictions? The Bible stands alone in these regards. Or consider second, its amazing impact on world history. Consider the manifest impact of the Bible on art, science, literature, culture, and law, or take a famous occurrence in the late nineteenth century. A prominent atheist in England challenged a well-known street preacher to debate. The preacher accepted with one qualification: In addition to their prepared arguments, each side would also have to produce fifty citizens who, prior to embracing the teaching, lived lives of dissolution and pain but now, having embraced their point of view, are model, upright citizens. The atheist balked. The preacher said, "Okay, twenty. No? How about ten? Five? Okay, I'll debate you if you can produce one life that has been transformed for the good by your atheism." With that, the professor canceled the debate.

We could go on to talk about why anything is "wrong." If there is "wrong," then we must know the opposite, "right"; and if so, who decides what is "right"? There must be a "Law Maker" in the universe. Otherwise, we talk nonsense, and the survival of the fittest should be the only arbitrator of behavior.

Over the centuries, philosophers have hammered out rules for logical communication. A famous example is that, in logical reasoning, "A" cannot be "A" and "non-A" at the same time. (Therefore, "Draw me a round triangle" is an "illogical" request.) Another famous principle is that of "falsifiability." In order for something to be considered "provable," you have to be able to imagine an experiment that the hypothesis can pass or fail. What about my belief that the Bible is the Word of God and that the God of the Bible exists? Is that a "logical" belief? Is it "falsifiable"?

I would say yes! There are several teachings in Scripture that provide a test. For instance, Jesus said, "For you always have the poor with you." (John 12:8) Therefore, if there is ever a time on planet Earth when there are no more poor people, then we could say that the Bible has been proven wrong. In Jeremiah 31, God promises to never forget or forsake His people, the Jews. If there comes a time in human history when there are no more Jews on the planet, then the Bible would be proven wrong. All four Gospels proclaim that Jesus of Nazareth rose from the dead. All the authorities of the first century had to do was produce His body to prove the rumor false.

Let me conclude by saying that I believe in God because the book we call the Bible says He exists and tells me what He has done, is going to do, and will do in the future; and that book has gripped my mind and won't let me go. The power of that communication by itself is my "proof."

Thinking about this truth, the words of Dr. Francis Schaeffer, the founder of L'Abri Fellowship in the village of Huemoz in the Swiss Alps, are challenging, when he said, "Now let me express this in a couple of other ways. One way to say it is that without the infinite-personal God, the God of personal unity and diversity, there is no answer to the existence of what exists. We can say it in another way, however, and that is that the infinite-personal God, the God who is Trinity, has spoken. He is there, and he is not silent. There is no use having a silent God. We would not know anything about Him. He has spoken and told us what He is, and He existed before all else, and so we have the answer to the existence of what are the consequences of one who rejects the very existence of God?."[1]

The apostle Paul wrote to the church in Rome:

"For the wrath of God is revealed from heaven against all ungodliness and unrighteousness of men, who hold the truth in unrighteousness; Because that which may be known of God is manifest in them; for God hath shewed it unto them. For the invisible things of him from the creation of the world are clearly seen, being understood by the things that are made, even his eternal power and Godhead; so that they are without excuse: Because that, when they knew God, they glorified him not as God, neither were thankful; but became vain in their imaginations, and their foolish heart was darkened. Professing themselves to be wise, they became fools, and changed the glory of the uncorruptible God into an image made like to corruptible man, and to birds, and fourfooted beasts, and creeping things." (Romans 1: 18-23)

Here, he speaks of the wrath of God is (being) revealed from heaven against all ungodliness and unrighteousness of men, who hold (hold down, suppress) the truth in unrighteousness.

How can this be? It is because of what we read in verses 19, 20.

"Because that which may be known of God is manifest in them; for God hath shewed it unto them. For the invisible things of him from the creation of the world are clearly seen, being understood by the things that are made, even his eternal power and Godhead; so that they are without excuse."

The word "wrath" in Greek is "ogre" and refers to a settled attitude against evil.

Thayer says, in his exegesis from the Greek, this anger or wrath arises gradually. The idea is God's wrath is not a childlike temper tantrum but His settled attitude against evil.

Some say, "How can a God of love have wrath?" Trench, the great Greek scholar, answering this penetrating question, said, "God could not love good, unless He hates evil. The two are inseparable, for you must do both or neither."

In conclusion, I would say that not only through the voice of conscience and the voice of creation, but also lastly and most importantly through God's immutable canon, the proof is clear. There is a God, and He has communicated to man.

Chapter Two

Simple but Profound: Going beyond Theism to Personal Monotheism

As one given to theology and evangelism, I am committed to keeping the message clear and biblically correct. Describing the plan of God's salvation is my passion and, by the grace of God, has been a successful endeavor in my life. In this chapter, however, I will not seek to evangelize but rather to theologically explain salvation. How does the Bible describe God's plan of salvation and how, therefore, should we understand how salvation works?

Some definitions and clarifications are in order. I do not consider myself to be a "religious" person because I do not consider my spiritual experiences to be the result of an encounter with "religion." "Religion" is what man does to approach God. In "religion," God has to be appeased by man's behavior. In Scripture, I find that man can do nothing to please God. Therefore, I do not have a "religion"; I have a "relationship" with God wherein He does all that is necessary to save me. In this same vein, I can continue by saying that I do not have "ritual" but "reality," not "ceremony" but "certainty."

If asked what my "religion" is, I will answer "Christian" in some settings to avoid immediate confusion. However, I will eventually need to qualify both the "religion" concept and also the "Christian" concept. The word "Christian" is a wonderful word. It literally means "little Christ," which is an amazing concept of what we should be in this world. Yet the word "Christian" only appears three times in the Bible: Acts 11:26, Acts 26: 28, and 1 Peter 4:16. In each instance, suffering and persecution are in view. However, "Christianity" has been altered through the centuries to the point that many branches of Christianity no longer follow the original teachings of Christ. I refer to them as "Christendom." To qualify my own Christianity, I will specify that I am a "born-again evangelical Christian." Nor would I avoid the title "born-again fundamental Christian," even though the modern media has turned "fundamentalism" into a derisive term.

Saving Faith

These definitions and clarifications bring me to a unique starting point for our discussion of how salvation works. All the religions in the history of the world, including many of the branches of Christendom, depend on human effort for sins to be forgiven and the sinner admitted into God's heaven. Evangelical Christianity (and the biblical theology of Judaism that it is founded on) is the only "religion" in human history in which God does everything necessary to provide the opportunity for salvation. It is the only religion in which God sacrifices Himself, dying in place of sinful mankind, becoming one of them as a substitute.

"For he hath made him to be sin for us, who knew no sin; that we might be made the righteousness of God in him." (2 Corinthians 5:21)

That is the plan and provision for salvation. How is it appropriated by individual humans? The answer is, and always has been, "We receive what God has provided for us by faith."

It is easy to look at the 613 laws in the Law of Moses, of which 248 were positive commands and 365 negative commands, and assume that these rules were designated for humans to obey in order to merit their salvation. That, however, is never taught in the Bible. On the contrary, in Genesis 15, we are informed that Abraham "believed in the Lord; and he counted it to him for righteousness." This was years before Abraham was circumcised, the ultimate marker of Jewishness in the Law of Moses, and before the institution of the Mosaic Law. Consistently throughout Scripture, the emphasis is on man needing to take God at His Word when He offers free salvation. Our only response is "yes" or "no."

Here are a few other passages that emphasize the ease with which salvation can be received:

"For this commandment which I command thee this day, it is not hidden from thee, neither is it far off. It is not in heaven, that thou shouldest say, Who shall go up for us to heaven, and bring it unto us, that we may hear it, and do it? Neither is it beyond the sea, that thou shouldest say, Who shall go over the sea for us, and bring it unto us, that we may hear it, and do it? But the word is very nigh unto thee, in thy mouth, and in thy heart, that thou mayest do it." (Deuteronomy 30:11-14)

"Ho, every one that thirsteth, come ye to the waters, and he that hath no money; come ye, buy, and eat; yea, come, buy wine and milk without money and without price. Wherefore do ye spend money for that which is not bread? and your labour for that which satisfieth not? hearken diligently unto me, and eat ye that which is good, and let your soul delight itself in fatness. Incline your ear, and come unto me: hear, and your soul shall live; and I will make an everlasting covenant with you, even the sure mercies of David. Behold, I have given him for a witness to the people, a leader and commander to the people. Behold, thou shalt call a nation that thou knowest not, and nations that knew not thee shall run unto thee because of the Lord thy God, and for the Holy One of Israel; for he hath glorified thee. Seek ye the Lord while he may be found, call ye upon him while he is near." (Isaiah 55:1-6)

"Behold, his soul which is lifted up is not upright in him: but the just shall live by his faith." (Habakkuk 2:4)

"But as many as received him, to them gave he power to become the sons of God, even to them that believe on his name . . ." (John 1:12)

That faith is the only requirement seems to be a simple concept, but humans traditionally stumble over the idea. In some cases, it is a result of pride. We are certain that we are able to do something to merit favor with God and, therefore, want to do so to receive the acclaim of both God and man.

Others argue that we actually do nothing for salvation, not even believe, because believing would be a human effort as well. They argue that God sovereignly declares who will be saved and then gives faith to those individuals as He regenerates them (the "born again" experience). They claim that Ephesians 2:8, 9 teaches that "faith" is the "gift of God" given to humans for salvation. Terms are coined to express these concepts: "Monergism" means that salvation is "one-sided"—God does it all from beginning to end. "Synergism" means that salvation is "two-sided"—God and man cooperate in the salvation process. I am monergistic as to the provision of salvation (man can do nothing to provide for the forgiveness of sins), but I am synergistic as it relates to the appropriation of salvation (man must say "yes" to receive).

I note that in Ephesians 2:8, 9 the pronouns are neuter, but the word "faith" is feminine. Therefore, what is given ("For by grace are ye saved through faith; and that not of yourselves: *it is* the gift of God: not of works, lest any man should boast.") is not the feminine faith but rather the general (neuter) concept of salvation. Salvation is the gift, but it is "our faith" that responds to God. James would agree with the assessment in that he argues that "faith without works is dead." He clearly does not consider "faith" to be "work." The concept is that true saving faith will produce works at some time and in some way.

Perhaps it would help to remember that "faith" is not an object. It is a response from a free-willed intelligent being. The Bible speaks of "our" faith (Matthew 9:29; 1 Corinthians 15:14). I agree that the world, the flesh, and the devil have triply blinded sinful humans. Therefore, God does have to convict, enlighten, draw, and soften a sinner's heart; but there eventually comes a point when the sinner sees the issue clearly and must respond to receive salvation. He must respond to God's provision for man's salvation, which is the sacrificial death of the resurrected Son of God.

The Content of Saving Faith

Another issue to consider is the content of saving faith. What does an individual need to know and believe in to become a saved person?

Paul defines the Gospel for us in 1 Corinthians 15:3-4: "For I delivered unto you first of all that which I also received, how that Christ died for our sins according to the Scriptures; and that he was buried, and that he rose again the third day according to the Scriptures."

The center of the Gospel of the grace of God is the death, burial, and resurrection of Christ. Therefore, when I preach, I do not just talk about Christ dying on the cross to wash away our sins but conclude the process with the burial and resurrection. Beyond this, we can argue that the Christ who is seen dying on the cross must be viewed as God in the flesh. Otherwise, His sin-bearing was not sufficient to wash away our sins. God is an infinite person. One human sin is of infinite guilt. That is why humans cannot pay for their own sin. They owe infinite payment.

Therefore, the sin bearer has to be an infinite person—God in the flesh dying in our place as our substitute.

The Gospel message of the grace of God must include not only the good news of God's provision, but also the bad news of man's sin and condition before a Holy God. There is no conversion without conviction of sin.

Lordship Salvation

An issue that has troubled me as I have watched the progress of evangelism over the last fifty years is the concept of "discipleship" and "Lordship." Some well-meaning individuals have been disturbed by those who preach and witness just for numbers' sake. Critics say that people talk others into making some sort of outward response to a simple message and that they count that external response as a conversion without stopping to see if the person understands the basics of salvation or the nature of the response that is sought. The sad truth is that a lot of these critics have never personally shared with a single person, one on one, the precious Gospel of the grace of God. The crucial issue in sharing the Gospel is to make sure the hearer understands his sinful, lost condition and that the only remedy of this plight is receiving God's gift of eternal life and the forgiveness of sin by faith alone in Christ alone. We must keep the message clear and not complicate it by unbiblical additions. Moses cried out to the people of Israel in the wilderness after they were bitten by the fiery serpents, "Look and live!" It is simple but very profound.

Some who have been disturbed by what they call the oversimplification of the presentation of the Gospel have gone to an extreme to "protect" evangelism. They claim that a person's salvation experience can only come after an extensive introduction into the basics of Christian theology. The individual must understand that to accept salvation is also to accept the rigors of discipleship. According to them, the individual must understand that "Lord" is not just "Jehovah" but also the "Master of my life from now on." If a person is deficient in any of these areas of knowledge or understanding, they are in danger of not having a true salvation experience. Doing so, they rip certain texts from the context to defend their position. Some have wrongly presented the "rich young ruler" to inflate man's position. I have heard others mishandle the parables of the mysteries of the kingdom in Matthew 13, using them to make reference to eternal salvation. This is especially true with the parable of "the pearl of great price," in which they say we must sell all that we have to get all that Christ is. The problem is that we do not purchase salvation; it is a gift (Titus 3:5). And Christ is not for sale.

The unfortunate result of this reaction is to make salvation something that appears to require work to merit salvation. The picture it conveys is a person cleaning up his life in preparation for the privilege to receive Christ as Savior. Of greater concern, we seem to be asking the person to have thoughts and attitudes about Christ and sin that only the indwelling Holy Spirit can produce. He has to be working inside of the person for him to draw those conclusions.

I conclude, therefore, that "Lord" is a reference to Jesus's deity, not primarily a statement that the sinner is agreeing to make Him the Master of his life before salvation can occur. Once he is born again and the Holy Spirit is guiding the sanctification (growth) process, he will then consider the claims of Christ's mastery over every area of his life. I feel the same about "discipleship." I do not consider "discipleship" to be a synonym for "salvation." John 6:66 talks about "disciples" who went back and walked with Him no longer. Therefore, "disciple" is not the equivalent to a "saved person." The call to discipleship can only be permanently accepted and implemented in the life of a saved individual who is being guided by the indwelling Holy Spirit. It involves the growth process of the believer otherwise known as sanctification.

Another discussion that is often included in the "lordship salvation" debate is the nature of "repentance." Those who want to include "Master" in the definition of "Lord" also teach that to truly make Christ "Master" involves consciously planning to give up every habitual sin in the salvation process. Since some sins are less obvious than others, the lordship salvationist frequently wants the individual to be in a Bible study for a period for these sins to become obvious before inviting him to make a commitment to Christ. Again, we are expecting the sin-darkened individual to understand issues that are only understandable by the redeemed mind influenced by the illumination of the indwelling Holy Spirit. In effect, it seems as though we are encouraging sinners to clean up their lives before trusting Christ as their personal Savior.

The main word for "repent" in the New Testament means "change of mind." I view this to be general, not pinpointing every type of sin. As an unsaved person, I wasn't sure if there was a God. I didn't understand that

His Son became a man and died in my place to take the punishment for my sins. I did not know that He rose from the dead. I did know that my behavior was not pleasing to God, if He existed, but that didn't matter to me. However, as the Word of God began to convict me and I began to understand certain realities, I came to the place of repentance. I repented in the sense that I changed my mind. Now I thought that there was a God. I understood the He sent His Son to die in my place. I understood that He was buried and rose again, indicating that His death had been accepted as a payment for sins. I understood that my sinfulness separated me from this Holy God, and I was sorry for that sin, wanting to be forgiven. All these changes in my thinking were acts of repentance.

The conclusion comes from a lack of understanding the use of the word "repent" in Scripture. It is important to ask the question "Repent from what?" Also, it is interesting to note that the word "repent" is used in reference to God Himself. Genesis 6:6 says, "And it repented the Lord that he had made man on the earth, and it grieved him at his heart." All would agree that God did not have to repent of sin.

The word "repent" was also used in extra-biblical literature. Dr. Charles Ryrie, in his book *So Great Salvation*, quoted R. C. Trench, referring to a passage from Plutarch in which two murderers who have spared a child afterward repented (*metenosean*) and tried to slay it. He also cites another instance in which *metameleia* (another word for "repent," also used in the New Testament) is used in the same sense of repenting of something good to do something bad. Notice that both these examples involved a change of mind about something good, not about sin. After the repentance, sinful things were done.[1]

Even Christians are called on to repent as we see in the word of the resurrected, glorified Christ to the churches in Asia Minor in Revelation 2 and 3, and it is used in the plural sense in most cases. There are more examples in Scripture that do not refer to eternal salvation. When repentance is used in reference to eternal salvation, it is never a two-step requirement for salvation. I have heard many well-meaning evangelists say, "You must repent of your sins and believe in Christ." It is not "repent and believe" that brings one to eternal salvation. As a matter of fact, "repent" and "believe" are synonyms in certain biblical texts. The word "repent" does not appear once in the Gospel of John, but various forms of "believe" appear over ninety times.

The very purpose of the Gospel of John is to bring one to saving faith.

But these are written, that ye might believe that Jesus is the Christ, the Son of God; and that believing ye might have life through his name (John 20:31).

It is also important to see Acts 20:21 repentance as two sides of the same coin. This reminds me of the old perforated train tickets that carried on them a word of caution stating, "Invalid if detached." If we make repentance as cleaning up our lives, we are practically saying that we must clean up our lives before we can believe and be saved. My friend, that makes it a works salvation. Biblical saving faith includes a change of mind and heart about the person of Christ and our own sinful state.

God's Sovereignty and Man's Free Will/Responsibility

Another issue that has an impact on the content of the Gospel is the whole issue of God's sovereignty in human events and man's free will/responsibility. In this centuries-old discussion, some have emphasized the sovereignty of God to the point that man's free will and responsibility in the present day are negated. (I suppose they would argue that man was created with free will, but with the fall man, free will has been lost. It is trapped by sin and Satan, and therefore, God has to do everything in relation to salvation.) Those who take this strict view would argue that God has to regenerate the sinner (the "born again" experience) before the sinner can evidence the faith that God also gives him (the Ephesians 2:8, 9 discussion). The final bit of logic they apply to this scenario is that God, knowing who He intended to regenerate would, therefore, only have His Son die for those so designated.

While you can see how they might take some isolated statements in Scripture to support this logic, the sweeping story of Scripture from Genesis 1:1 to Revelation 22:22 does not allow it to stand.

John 3:16-19 makes it clear that the center point of discussion is the sin of unbelief. Scripture is clear that God is a "just" and "fair" individual. It is impossible for God to be "just" and "fair" if He condemns people to eternal punishment for refusing to believe in a death that Christ did not die for them. Christ had to have died for all if some of the all are sent to hell for not believing that He died for all. In 1 John 2:2, it is made clear that He is the propitiation for the sins of the whole world.

While God certainly is sovereign in the creation of His plan and certainly has the power to do whatever He wants (consistent with

His nature), it is also manifestly clear in Scripture that the sovereign God decreed that man have a free will, not just at the beginning but throughout human history. Therefore, while God makes all the provisions for salvation and is actively working for free-willed individuals to understand salvation, there comes a point in the sinner's education process when he must use his free will to say yes to God. At this point, I understand the statement that man is "dead" in sins not to mean "unconscious" or "unaware" but rather "separated from God." Therefore, the "dead" sinner does not have to be "regenerated" ("made alive") in order to believe, but rather, as God illumines the sinner's mind and he responds in faith, his faith becomes the trigger that allows the Holy Spirit to regenerate him. God does not force the human will in that He longs for free-willed individuals who will love Him of their own free wills.

It is also important to note that the word "believe" from the Greek text is in the aorist active imperative tense. What does that mean, you ask. It means a completed choice to believe is in a command form. That means the jailor was personally commanded to believe at that moment. Here is a question: "Is it just for God to command man to do something that he is incapable of doing?"

Election

"What about 'election'?" some would reply. This is another controversial aspect of the process of salvation. The Bible never identifies the basis of God's designation of the "elect." However, frequently, the emphasis of "election" is not in the "entry into salvation" but rather the consequences of the saved state. We are "elected" to "sonship" or to service. He "elected" Israel, but many within the "elect" never got saved. The "elect" nation, however, was "elect" to accomplish several spiritual tasks: (1) to be a witness to the Gentile world, (2) to be the biological line of the Messiah, and (3) to be the writers of the Old Testament and New Testament.

On the flip side, some in Scripture whom we might identify as the "non-elect" actually "elected" themselves to that status. Ten times in Exodus we are told that the pharaoh had a hard heart. Five times the passages imply that God hardened his heart. Five times it says that the pharaoh hardened his heart. The matter is solved by divine revelation in 1 Samuel 6:6, where the Holy Spirit explains that the pharaoh first hardened his heart: "Why then do you harden you hearts as the Egyptians and Pharaoh hardened their hearts?"

Romans 9:21-23 is often used to justify a fatalistic understanding of election:

Hath not the potter power over the clay, of the same lump to make one vessel unto honor, and another unto dishonor? What if God, willing to shew his wrath, and to make his power known, endured with much longsuffering the vessels of wrath fitted to destruction: And that he might make known the riches of his glory on the vessels of mercy, which he had afore prepared unto glory.

It is crucial to note that this statement comes not in a discussion of personal salvation but rather in the larger discussion of God choosing the line of Jacob ("Israel") over the line of Esau ("Edomites")—with "believers" (elect) and "non-believers" (non-elect) in both lines through history. As the discussion continues through Romans 10 and 11, Paul is going to conclude that while God has set aside Israel for the time being to work with the church, He will eventually restore that line to its original place of blessedness.

In Romans 9:22, the Greek verb in the phrase "vessels of wrath prepared for destruction" can be either in the middle voice or the passive voice (for this verb, the endings are the same). The verse can, therefore, be understood as "prepared themselves for destruction" (if understood in the middle voice) or "were prepared for destruction" (if understood in the passive voice) without specifying that "God did it." In stark contrast, in Romans 9:23, Paul uses the active voice, saying, *God prepared* the vessels of mercy.

The application to personal election would be "God prepares those people who believe for eternal blessedness" while "those who refuse to believe prepare themselves for eternal destruction." Our expression of the sovereignty of God can never take away from human responsibility for the simple reason that a just God will only punish rational beings for transgressions that are their own fault.

I have been constantly impressed with the fact that the apostle Paul, who might be considered a strict voice for the sovereignty of God in Scripture, nevertheless preached, witnessed, and prayed as though it was his responsibility to woo men and women to God. He would be the first to give God the credit but the last to stop preaching, lest they not have a proper chance to consider the claims of Christ. If pressed, I suppose I would insist that God's "elects" in the sense that He knows how men and women will respond to His offer of salvation and from His timeless perspective identifies them as "those who would trust in Him" with the designation "the elect" (1 Peter 1:2).

Although some would hold that foreknowledge simply means a previous relationship, this is hard to prove in every case in Scripture. The theological argument is that of conditional or unconditional election. But it is important to note that even God conditions Himself in accord with His divine plan. This is not a conflict with His sovereignty. He is sovereign in the plan and the form of its implementation.

Chapter Three

Finding Your Place: How to Find Your Place in Life

Finding Your Place

Have you ever stopped to wonder what place God has for you in life? It's important to understand that he has something specific in mind for each one of us and wants us to know and do His will.

We should often ask ourselves throughout our lives where we are in the plan of God. We need to understand that to live outside of God's purpose can only lead to frustration and heartache.

For we are his workmanship, created in Christ Jesus unto good works, which God hath before ordained that we should walk in them. (Ephesians 2:10)

The word "workmanship" in Greek is "poiema," from the word "poiseo," which means "I make it," only found in Ephesians 2:10 and in Romans 1:20. Abbott-Smith defines the word as "a complete work," even the concept of handiwork. It denotes a masterpiece of art. I like what my good friend Andy Horner, the founder of Premier Designs, along with his wife Joan, says, "God does not make junk." We derive our English word "poem" from this word. Just as a good poem has rhyme, rhythm, and reason and is a reflection of the heart of its author, our Creator has this in mind for each believer. It is so moving for me to muse that my salvation is not an ending point but a starting point in God's great work to conform me with rhyme, rhythm, and reason into the image of Christ as we see in Romans 8:29.

It is sad to think that some people never find their place in life. They spend their days jumping from one thing to the next and never really experience the deep satisfaction of knowing that they're in the place that God has for them. The writer of Proverbs said it like this, "As a bird that wandereth from her nest, so is a man that wandereth from his place." (Proverbs 27:8)

What an amazing picture of the one who has lost direction in life.

This brief study will look at the matter of "finding your place" and will offer some biblical principles for following the plan that God has just for you.

Principles of Discovery

Many Christians ask, "How can I really know my place in life?"

The greatest adventure one can embark upon in life is to know God. This begins by placing your trust in Jesus Christ. The Bible teaches that He is the Son of God and that He offered Himself as a sacrifice to pay the penalty for our sins. You see, it is our sin that separates us from God. Not only did He die, but He rose again from the dead. His resurrection is the proof that God the Father found His sacrifice acceptable to satisfy God's righteous demands and remove our guilt from before Him. That is what paved the way for us to know Him.

The more we get to know God and the more we understand His mind, the more we will understand ourselves. This understanding is a lifelong pursuit, and knowing God should become such a thirst that it is never quenched. The psalmist expressed it this way:

As the hart (deer) panteth after the water brooks, so panteth my soul after thee, O God. (Psalm 42:1)

Knowing God: His Person

We come to know the person of God as we study His attributes in the Bible, the Word of God. The more we know of His attributes, the more vivid our understanding will be of what He is like. I would challenge you to spend time thinking about God and His attributes as they are revealed in His Word and through the person of Jesus Christ. (John 14:9).

Here are some examples of the attributes of God with which you can start:

A. *His goodness:* It was the goodness of God that Satan attacked in the Garden of Eden. There, he convinced Eve that God was withholding something because He did not have her best interest in mind. Essentially, he was saying that God was not good and could not be trusted.

The psalmist wrote, "O taste and see that the Lord is good: blessed is the man that trusteth in him." (Psalm 34:8)

Knowing God's goodness will allow you to face any storm in life with joy, knowing that God cares for you and only gives what is best.

B. *His wisdom:* The writer of Proverbs wrote, "The fear of the Lord is the beginning of wisdom: and the knowledge of the holy is understanding." (Proverbs 9:10)

The Hebrew word for "wisdom" is "chokmah" and speaks of skills and arts. It is fleshing out God's truth in my own spiritual walk. We see in this word keen insight into life and ways of dealing with its problems.

When we read of the fear of the Lord, we should not come to the conclusion that God wants us cowering in His presence, but rather, we are to understand it as a reverential awe of God. This reverential awe (fear) is the beginning of wisdom. When we recognize that God is wise, that He is smarter than the brightest of humanity, and we embrace the depth of His great wisdom, we will increase in our knowledge of God.

C. *His love:* The more we understand about God's love, the more we understand that we are not following some menacing deity, as painted by the pagan gods of secular culture, but we're walking with a God who loves and cares about each one of us.

Late in my teen years, thoughts of God's love really captured my heart. For those of us who have grown up in the difficult situation of an unbelieving and fearful home life, this knowledge of the love of God grips our souls. This truth only becomes a reality as we come to understand the person and character of God. In my own life, it was not until I became intensely involved in the study of God's Word that I really grasped God's love for me.

At the age of eighteen, I wrote the following, which I simply called *Poems to My Savior.*

"Fill Me"

Oh, bread of heaven,
I cried to thee
To fill my hungry soul.
Thou who art the splendor of all glory,
Light these darkened windows
of my earthen house
To be consumed with the ever-radiant glow
of thy molten Word.
Fill me, O God.

"Alone with My Love"
Alone with God, oh, joy divine,
Just to know that Jesus is mine.
My heart beats fast and begins to pound
When I venture to higher ground.
A word, a whisper to my Lover Divine,
Then all His beauty I behold is fine.
Looking to His flaming eyes sends me to the
fullness of rhapsody.
As He draws near, I suddenly see the marks of
love He bore for me.
Pierced hands, feet, and side,
O Jesus, it was for me you died.
My heart is humbled and starts to sink
As on my Savior's love I began to think.
"Oh, my Savior, why do you love me?" I ask.
But then I know I shall never know in this
earthly mask.
So I sigh and say to my Lord,
"Oh, Jesus, tie me to thy Lover's cords."

When you take this perspective, the Bible becomes more than just a book of academic pursuits; it becomes a love letter from a loving God. Knowing God—that He is good, that He is wise, that He is loving—will help you do what is right.

I have mentioned only three of the many attributes of God, but I can assure you that knowing God's attributes will help lay a firm foundation upon which you can build your life.

Knowing God: His Providence

In theology, *providence* is God's continual care and loving direction over His creation.

The prophet Isaiah wrote, "I am the Lord, and there is none else, there is no God beside me: I girded thee, though thou hast not known me." (Isaiah 45:5)

He wrote these words to a heathen king named Cyrus.

Even though Cyrus did not know God, His providence was at work in Cyrus's life. As I meditated on the word "girded" that is stated in Isaiah 45:5, my understanding of the text and God's great work was opened. It comes from the Hebrew word "azor," which means properly to wrap around one's loins as attire on the arms. Figuratively, it comes from the idea of fully equipped and clothed with strength to meet challenges head on. This is God's great work of providence and goes beyond my feeble understanding.

God is at work in your life too, whether you know it or not. As you are finding your place in life, what an awesome thought it is to know that God's work did not begin with your salvation but can be traced back even before you were in your mother's womb.

The psalmist said it like this:

"For thou hast possessed my reins: thou hast covered me in my mother's womb. I will praise thee; for I am fearfully and wonderfully made: marvellous are thy works; and that my soul knoweth right well. My substance was not hid from thee, when I was made in secret, and curiously wrought in the lowest parts of the earth. Thine eyes did see my substance, yet being unperfect; and in thy book all my members were written, which in continuance were fashioned, when as yet there was none of them. How precious also are thy thoughts unto me, O God! How great is the sum of them!" (Psalm 139:13-17)

And "He fashioneth their hearts alike; he considereth all their works." (Psalm 33:15)

The word "fashioned" brings the idea of molding or an intricate work of the Maker.

And how about these words by that great servant of God, the apostle Paul: "Paul, a servant of Jesus Christ, called to be an apostle, separated unto the Gospel of God." (Romans 1:1)

Paul understood that he was chosen by God to preach the Gospel, but when did this happen? Did it occur when he met the Lord on the Damascus Road? Note these words from the book of Galatians:

"But when it pleased God, who separated me from my mother's womb, and called me by his grace . . ." (Galatians 1:15).

Providence is a treasured, timeless truth. Merill Unger wrote, "The constant and final aim of God's providence is the fulfillment of His purpose . . . How broad and wonderful, and this may defy our human comprehension."

We need to know God—His person, His providence, His power.

Knowing God: His Power

Paul wrote to the Ephesians, "Now unto him that is able to do exceeding abundantly above all that we ask or think, according to the power that worketh in us." (Ephesians 3:20)

This is Paul's doxology. The phrase "exceeding abundantly above" brings with it the concept of exhaustlessness. My Lord's ability goes beyond all human comprehension. The phrase "exceeding abundantly" is a doubly compounded word, meaning "super abundantly," which is used only here and then in 1 Thessalonians 3:10 and 5:13, and speaks of the limitless power of the Holy Spirit of God.

Thirty years after Paul's conversion, we see his unceasing desire to know in full measure and personally the experience of the power of Christ's resurrection in his life. I believe one of the reasons God used Jack Wyrtzen in such great ways, which shook his generation, was that the power of resurrection of the living Christ was so evident in his life.

When you get to know God and His person, His providence, and His power, you will walk through life with direction instead of wandering aimlessly through your days.

It is important that we know God, but we also must know some things about ourselves.

A. Know yourself

Be honest with yourself. Do not just be a wishful thinker. Here are a few things to consider:

God uses different people in different scenarios to bring us to salvation. God brought me from Lakeland, Florida, all the way to Word of Life Island in Schroon Lake, New York. It was there that I put my faith in Jesus Christ after hearing the Gospel, and it was all a part of His divine plan.

As you think about your life, how has God's plan unfolded in your salvation? It doesn't end there. God wants to use you to serve Him and others. He has given you a spiritual gift to discover and then develop. Remember, you're not an island—you have a part in God's universal plan. One of the great blessings of the Christian life is to rub shoulders with other brothers and sisters in Christ. As you do, you will minister to them, and they will have a part in your life and maturity.

Paul said it like this:

"But speaking the truth in love, may grow up into him in all things, which is the head, even Christ: From whom the whole body fitly joined together and compacted by that which every joint supplieth, according to the effectual working in the measure of every part, maketh increase of the body unto the edifying of itself in love." (Ephesians 4:15-16)

And the wise man said, "Iron sharpeneth iron; so a man sharpeneth the countenance of his friend." (Proverbs 27:17)

Your life and service to Christ is a great benefit to others in the church, the body of Christ. You need to find your place so that you can fulfill your part in the awesome universal plan of God.

B. Know true satisfaction

What is it that gives you deep, lasting fulfillment in your service for Christ? I think some people have given the impression that serving God is something you must endure. That is wrong. Serving God is something you should enjoy. Often you encounter people who will belittle a life of service, but don't let them dissuade you. Serving God is awesome and is a place of great joy.

C. Know your world

Not *the* world, but *your* world. As we minister the Word of God, we handle God's timeless, *unchanging* truths, but we live in a *changing* world. Nevertheless, the changes are not internal but external. These can be certain changes of fashion but not in fact.

Harry Ironside said many times, "If it is true it is not new, and if it is new it is not true."

What was he talking about? He was referring to essence, not expression. There must be an understanding of style and substance.

As Jack Wyrtzen said, "I believe every generation must reach their generation for Christ."

The world in which we live is constantly changing. When I was young, television was just being introduced. When my wife and I began on the mission field, communication with the home office was by telegram. Today we live in a high-tech world, but man's basic problems remain the same. It still is the Word of God that holds the answers to our essential needs. This is an exciting time in which to live because people are looking for answers, and answers can only be found in God's Word.

The events of September 11 were catastrophic, but there is a greater catastrophe occurring daily in our world, as people are entering into an eternity without hope because they do not know Jesus Christ. My prayer is that God will ignite a passion in your soul to be a source of light in the midst of this present dark age.

D. Know your spiritual gifts

A spiritual gift is a God-given ability to serve Christ and His body, the church. These abilities are received at the moment of belief, as we see in Ephesians 1:3, "Blessed be the God and Father of our Lord Jesus Christ, who hath blessed us with all spiritual blessings in heavenly places in Christ."

These spiritual gifts help us determine where we fit in God's program of perfecting the saints in the work of the ministry for the edifying of the body of Christ.

> "And he gave some, apostles; and some, prophets;
> and some, evangelists; and some, pastors and teachers; for
> the perfecting of the saints, for the work of the ministry,

for the edifying of the body of Christ: Till we all come in
the unity of the faith, and of the knowledge of the Son of
God, unto a perfect man, unto the measure of the stature
of the fulness of Christ." (Ephesians 4:11-13)

Perils of Detour

When we do not follow the principles of discovery, we will inevitably
fall into the perils of detour; and like a bird that wonders from her nest,
we will suffer the consequences.

"As a bird that wandereth from her nest, so is a man
that wandereth from his place." (Proverbs 27:8)

Everything we have looked at so far brings us to the question "What
about the one who does not find his place?"

Consider what is lost by those who never find their place in God's
program.

A. **Loss of safety.** A bird that wonders from its nest seldom returns
without injury.

In the parable of the prodigal son (Luke 15), the son lost his place
of security. When you step out of God's will, you step onto a highway
of danger. It is interesting to know that anything that the prodigal son
sought outside of the will of God was only realized when he was in his
place in the will of God.

The psalmist wrote, "How excellent is thy lovingkindness, O God!
Therefore the children of men put their trust under the shadow of thy
wings." (Psalm 36:7)

How wonderful to have God's "hesed," loyal love, even when I
am not always loyal! But what does it mean to put our trust under the
shadow of Thy wings? For me, the word "shadow" brings with it the idea
of resting in God's divine knowledge and promises. The enemy will try to
attack me, but I will abide in the shadow of my God's wings.

B. **Loss of sustenance.** In the parable of the prodigal son, the
prodigal was starving (Luke 15:17), yet in his father's house, there
was plenty. The point is not that Christians never suffer, many

do, but rather, hardships often come when we stray outside of the plan of God for us.

The psalmist wrote, "I have been young, and now am old; yet have I not seen the righteous forsaken, nor his seed begging bread." (Psalm 37:25)

C. **Loss of strength.** A bird out of its nest is not at rest. Those who do not settle in the plan of God endure the same kind of stress, flying from one place to the next and never finding the place of rest. Restful service in God's place is awesome.

Jesus said, "Come unto me, all ye that labour and are heavy laden, and I will give you rest. Take my yoke upon you, and learn of me; for I am meek and lowly in heart: and ye shall find rest unto your souls. For my yoke is easy, and my burden is light." (Matthew 11:28-30)

And again, we read, "There remaineth therefore a rest to the people of God . . . Let us labour therefore to enter into that rest, lest any man fall after the same example of unbelief." (Hebrew 4:9, 11)

D. **Loss of spiritual impact.** Most people want to get to the end of their days and be able look back and see that their life mattered, that they had an impact.

Paul wrote, "Not as though I had already attained, either were already perfect: but I follow after, if that I may apprehend that for which also I am apprehended of Christ Jesus." (Philippians 3:12)

If you never find and settle in the place God has for you, then it will be hard to ever have a lasting impact. Most work of great and lasting value does not happen overnight.

E. **Loss of satisfaction.** A man out of his place is never satisfied. For the one who knows true satisfaction, it is never his circumstances that make the difference.

Harry Ironside, one of the great Bible teachers the past century, had these words spoken by David Livingston written in the flyleaf of his Bible: "I will place no value on anything I have, or may possess, except as it relates to the kingdom of Christ."

Jim Elliott, the missionary martyr to the Auca Indians, wrote, "God, I pray Thee light these idle candles in my life that I may burn for Thee.

Consume my life my God, it is Thine. I seek not a long life but a full one like You, Lord Jesus."

God's place for Jim Elliot was a lonely jungle in Ecuador and an early death, yet in God's service, he found deep satisfaction.

Finding your place in the plan of God begins with knowing God and then understanding yourself and the world in which God has placed you. My prayer is that you will be just where God wants you to be, that you will experience the most fulfilling pilgrimage that a man or woman could ever have, and that you will spend your days in glory in the grace of God.

> "As a bird that wandereth from her nest, so is a man
> that wandereth from his place." (Proverbs 27:8)

Chapter Four

Don't Bite the Bait: How You Can Have Triumph over Temptation

Temptation is an inescapable fact in the life of every believer.

The apostle Paul, to the first-century church in Corinth, wrote, "There hath no temptation taken you but such as is common to man: but God is faithful, who will not suffer you to be tempted above that ye are able; but will with the temptation also make a way to escape, that ye may be able to bear it." (1 Corinthians 10:13)

From this and other important portions of the Word of God, we can learn much that will help us stand when temptation knocks at our door. In this study, we will see six essential truths concerning temptation.

Temptation Is a Clear Principle

What is temptation? The first thing we need to understand is that temptation is not a sin. Temptation can result in sin if we yield to it. Experiencing temptation does not mean that you have sinned. In the Greek text, the word is "peirasmos" and can mean "a test" or "temptation." Here, it is important to understand that God does not tempt; He tests. It is Satan who tempts in the sense of a solicitation to evil.

God's testing is to raise us up; Satan's temptation is to throw us down. The test is a process that comes from God to make us more like Him. If we do not respond in a positive way to that test, it can be transformed into a temptation.

Dietrich Bonhoeffer was one of the great theological thinkers of the twentieth century. Imprisoned by the Nazis during World War II for helping a group of Jews escape to Switzerland, he was convicted of treason and put to death by hanging at the Flossenbürg concentration camp in 1945. During his imprisonment, Bonhoeffer wrote on many important doctrinal issues. One example is a brief paper he wrote on the subject of temptation. Read his words:

> *In our members there is a slumbering inclination toward desire which is both sudden and fierce. With irresistible power, desire seizes mastery over the flesh. All at once a secret smoldering fire is kindled. The flesh burns and is in flames. It makes no difference whether it is sexual desire or ambition or vanity or desire for revenge or love of fame and power or greed for money or finally, the strange desire for the beauty of the world of nature. Joy in God is in course of being extinguished within us and we seek all our joy in the creature at this moment. God is quite unreal to us. He loses all reality and only desire for the creature is real. The only reality is the devil. Satan does not fill us with hatred of God, but with forgetfulness of God. The lusts thus aroused envelop the mind and will of man in deepest darkness. The powers of clear discrimination and of decision are taken from us. It is here that everything within me rises up against the Word of God.*[1]

What a statement! To Bonhoeffer, even in a Nazi prison, he faced temptation. But what did he say about it? Bonhoeffer wrote of desire smoldering, trying to be kindled within us. What he was describing is the sin *nature* responding to the bait of temptation. He also noted that in the moment of temptation. God is quite unreal to us, we lose all reality of God, and we lapse into the forgetfulness of God. The temptations Bonhoeffer experienced during his time of sufferings in the Nazi camp goes against the Gnostic teaching that castigating the flesh purifies the spirit.

Temptation is not sin, but yielding to temptation is. Yielding to temptation is not a state of hating God but rather of forgetting God. Think about the times you've yielded to temptation. Temptation comes as a quiet voice whispering in your ear, and the reality of God seems to drift away like a ship drifting from its port. At that time, God seems distant.

Dag Hamershult wrote, "You cannot play with the animal in you without becoming wholly animal. You cannot play with falsehood without forfeiting your right to truth; play with cruelty without losing your sensitivity of mind. He who wants to keep his garden tidy doesn't reserve a plot for weeds." What a powerful image! So in principle, the reality of temptation is very clear, and we must be prepared.

Temptation Is a Common Problem

Look again at the portion of Scripture Paul wrote to the church at Corinth. We read, "There hath no temptation taken you but such as is common to man…"

There is a tendency for some to think that temptation is only for the young and the carnal; only for those who are weak and wimpy on their faith. But God says, through the apostle Paul, that temptation is a common problem.

Stop and think about some of the men in the Bible who faced temptation. Imagine David, the great king of Israel, as he walks on his rooftop in the afternoon and sees Bathsheba. This is a familiar example of temptation. Then there's Samson, who is tempted by Delilah, or you might think of Job. Do remember that God asked Satan, "Hast thou considered my servant Job that there is none like him?" The book of Job records the account of how he faced great temptation. Joseph, who was sold into slavery, is another example. Alone in the house of Potiphar, pursued by Potiphar's wife, Joseph faced temptation.

Even though Christ was impeccable, the test He faced was real. Yet for Him, it was a test not to see if He would sin, but to show that He could not sin. When we think of Jesus Christ and the test He faced, we remember the words of Hebrews 4:15: "For we have not an high priest which cannot be touched with the feeling of our infirmities; but was in all points tempted like as we are, yet without sin." Although He was impeccable, the test He faced was real; a test He passed flawlessly.

Every person who has ever lived has faced and will face temptation. Every person whom you and I know faces temptation. Temptation may come under a different guise, wearing a different mask; but it's the same old concept. It does not matter how young or old in your faith you are;

you will face temptation. It is a common problem, young or old, male or female. With this in mind, the study of this topic is so practical to each of us.

Years ago, I thought only men faced certain temptations and was astonished to learn that women faced them as well. But then it occurred to me that the Bible says it's "common to man!" Here, "man" is generic; in other words, it is saying "mankind" or "all people." It does not matter if you're rich or poor, young or old, male or female; it applies to all.

Temptation applies to the spiritual as well as carnal. The biblical examples just cited were made up of all kinds of people; some were spiritual, others were carnal, but all faced temptation.

We need to allow the Spirit of God to burn this on our heart: Temptation is not just something that happens in the first years of our Christian life; it is a foe we will face for the duration.

Temptation Is a Captivating Process

Captivation carries with it the idea of attraction or allurement. James says it like this: "Let no man say when he is tempted, I am tempted of God: for God cannot be tempted with evil, neither tempteth he any man: But every man is tempted, when he is drawn away of his own lust, and enticed." (James 1:13-14)

That little phrase "drawn away of his own lust and enticed" addresses the fact that the very presence of evil not only surrounds us, but it is also in us. We do have spiritual enemies—the world, the flesh, and the devil—all of which war against the believer. The word "enticed" carries the idea of bait being used to draw a fish out of the safety of its hiding place. The ironic thing we see from this passage is that the enticement comes from within. It is the image of a fish taking the bait, not realizing it covers a hook that will lead to it being caught, leading to its death.

What happens when the process follows its natural end, when the lust has conceived? It then brings forth sin; and sin, when it is finished, brings forth death.

John, in his first epistle, speaks about lust: "Love not the world, neither the things that are in the world. If any man love the world, the love of the Father is not in him. For all that is in the world, the lust of the flesh, and the lust of the eyes, and the pride of life, is not of the Father, but is of the world." (1 John 2:15-16)

The word "lust" in Greek text is "epithymia" and speaks of a passionate desire, which can be positive or negative. The word is used in a positive way in Luke 22:15, when He said to His disciples, "With great desire I have desired to eat this Passover with you before I suffer." In the negative sense, it is misplaced and a great danger. Strong desire does not purify what is unrighteous (i.e., outside of God's will and purpose for our lives).

The Shepherd of Hermas (first or second century AD) stated, "Remove every evil desire and clothe yourself with good and holy desire. For if you are clothed with good desire, you will hate evil desire, and it will be bridled."

Speaking about lust in the negative, Augustine said, "By lust, I mean that affection of the mind which aims at the enjoyment of oneself and one's neighbor without reference to God."

The lust of the flesh speaks of carnality; the lust of the eye, sensuality; the pride of life, vanity. We all have senses, such as seeing, hearing, feeling, and tasting, which are blessings from God, but the lust of the flesh goes beyond these; it is using these senses to please and gratify oneself instead of pleasing God. The eye gate, the ear gate, tasting and even feeling can all be avenues of sensuality. We live in a world that surrounds us with falsehood. The devil is a great impostor who substitutes lust and calls it love. He says something is right when it's wrong; that it is good when it's bad. The devil perverts everything from a beautiful body to a delightful pleasure and entices us to use them the wrong way. You see, the beautiful body is not the problem, and the delightful pleasure is not the problem. It's using them the wrong way; it's gratifying oneself in the wrong way, at the wrong time, or through the wrong source.

Sensuality is the core of vanity and promotes the attitude that says "I'm number one. I will do what I please. I will promote myself. I will pursue the things that elevate me in the eyes of my peers, even those who reject God."

Temptation Follows a Consistent Pattern

Temptation is a very captivating process, but it's not a new process; it's repeated again and again. The evil one is trying to captivate your mind, emotions, and will. Satan attacks your mind with thoughts, your emotions with feelings, and your will with decisions and choices.

The apostle Paul warned the church at Corinth, "Lest Satan should get an advantage of us: for we are not ignorant of his devices." (2 Corinthians 2:11)

Yes, the devil seeks a toe hold on the believer, and we are mandated to stop being ignorant of his devices, plot, or schemes.

My dear friend, not only does God have a plan for your life, but the devil also has a plan designed to take you down.

Also, he wrote to the Ephesians, "Put on the whole armour of God, that ye may be able to stand against the wiles of the devil." (Ephesians 6:11)

The word "devices" in 2 Corinthians 2:11 denotes "that which is purposed or planned." "Wiles" is akin to "craft" or "cunning." Both of these verses speak of Satan's pattern of attack. This pattern is tried and tested and, sadly, repeated over and over in our lives and all too frequently with success.

We saw in the previous section three avenues that Satan uses in temptation: the lust of the flesh, lust of the eyes, and the pride of life. Here, again, we see a consistent pattern emerge as he tempts in the areas of carnality, sensuality, and vanity.

Temptation Falls before a Concrete Promise

As we have looked thus far at this matter of temptation, the first four areas covered help us recognize and understand temptation. In the last two points, we will see that God has not left us defenseless.

The first thing we see is that in the midst of it all, there is a clear promise. In 1 Corinthians 10:13, we read, "There hath no temptation taken you but such as is common to man: but God is faithful."

God is faithful. Now there is a concrete promise. God *is* faithful.

Faithfulness is one of our Lord's divine characteristics.

In the Gospel of Luke, on the night before our Lord went to the cross, we see Him spending time in fellowship with His disciples. At that time, He turns to Peter and says, "And the Lord said, Simon, Simon, behold, Satan hath desired to have you, that he may sift you as wheat: But I have prayed for thee, that thy faith fail not: and when thou art converted, strengthen thy brethren." (Luke 22:31-32)

I love that!

Simon Peter had said, "Lord, though all desert you, not me! I'm the tough guy; I'll hang in there; I will not fail!"

Our Lord's reply is so interesting. Jesus calls him "Simon," not "Peter." "Peter" is "petros," a rock – like one. "Simon" is the fluctuating one! I believe Jesus looked into Peter's eyes with great love and told him that Satan desired (the word for a request that is granted) to sift him as wheat (to shake violently) but that He had prayed for him. God is so faithful. Would you allow the Spirit of God to burn that on your heart as we think about temptation? God is faithful. Jesus prayed for Peter that his faith would not fail.

Here, I don't believe that the Lord was praying that Peter wouldn't deny Him; He'd already said that he was going to do that. I think he was saying, "I am praying for you, that when you fail, you will not quit."

Today you may feel like the old tempter is saying to you, "Hey, throw in the towel! You blew it!" But God is faithful, and He's faithful to forgive. He's faithful to forget. He is faithful to fortify you. God is faithful. The faithfulness of God is your concrete promise throughout every temptation. So look to Him! It does not matter what problem, trial, or temptation you face—God is faithful.

Can I take you back to the life of Joseph? He was wrongfully imprisoned. Even after he gave the interpretation of the pharaoh's dreams, he was there for two years. But there, in that dungeon, God was faithful. God was with him, and He brought him out. That's awesome! God is going to bring you out too. The faithfulness of God, a concrete promise!

Temptation Affords a Constant Provision

What is provision? Provision is a way of escape. You see, the faithfulness of God will not allow any testing in your life that you cannot withstand. God has provided everything for you to have victory. This constant provision is a way to escape, a way that you may be able to go through or bear it. When we read 1 Corinthians 10:13 and come to the phrase "a way to escape," we think, "Ah, at last, the way out!" But as we look closer at the text, we see it says "a way to escape, that ye may be able to bear it." What we find is not a way *out* of the temptation but a way *through* the temptation. Think of it like this: When we face a time of testing and shoulder the weight of the trial, God is not going to allow us to buckle under the weight. But He is not going to just remove the weight either. In the time of testing, God comes alongside the believer and faithfully helps him endure the weight of the trial until he comes through that trial successfully.

God is not looking to pamper us but to perfect us.

James says, "My brethren, count it all joy when ye fall into divers temptations; knowing this, that the trying of your faith worketh patience. But let patience have her perfect work, that ye may be perfect and entire, wanting nothing." (James 1:2-4)

God has a purpose for the believer in enduring trials and wants to bring us through this process that we might emerge a mature and stable child of God, able to stand and withstand the wiles of the devil.

As we consider the person of God, we can trust in His goodness and His grace. As we face times of testing, there is a way out; but the way out is a way through. We have God's constant provision, and that provision first has its basis in His person.

I've talked to people around the world who say that their life is like a maze; they almost feel trapped. They go to one place and see an opening and then turn, only to find a wall. They just keep going around and around, wondering, "Where is the way out?" In times of trial, we must look to Jesus, the Author and Finisher of our faith. We must trust in the very person of God but also the very principles of God as found in the Word of God.

> "Thy Word have I hid in mine heart, that I might
> not sin against thee." (Psalm 119:11)

When I work with people who are constantly overcome by the same temptation, I encourage them to saturate their mind with Scripture dealing with the particular area in which they are struggling. Having done that when the temptation comes, the Word of God springs to their heart and mind, guiding them on how to do what is right in the sight of God.

We find God's provision in the person of God and the precepts of God but also in the people of God.

All believers need a friend that they can be open and candid with concerning the struggles that they face. We call this accountability, and the idea is completely biblical. One of the provisions God has given to us, as we seek to walk the Christian life, is our brothers and sisters in Christ.

With this in mind, let's help one another. Let's ask the hard questions, and let's answer them honestly. Let's join hands as we march to victory for the glory of God. As we face temptation, we must recognize there is a way of escape, and it is wrapped up in the constant provision of God.

As we conclude this brief study on temptation, there are some who may say, "Well, this sounds good, but I've already blown it. I've already yielded too much to temptation. I'm already so overcome that I don't know what to do."

I'm reminded of the great work of John Bunyan, *Pilgrim's Progress*. At one point, two of the characters in the story, Christian and Hopeful, fall asleep in a field that belongs to the giant called Despair. Despair takes them to Doubting Castle where he throws them into a cold, damp, and stinking dungeon. Trapped without food and water, the giant's wife proclaims, "Beat them! Tell them suicide!" In the dark moment, Christian reached into his pocket and found a key called promise. With that key, he opened the door of despair, the light flooded in, and they were freed from the giant of Despair.

Maybe you are in the dungeon of despair. It stinks, it's dark, and it's hopeless. Would you look deep into the pockets of your soul and pull out the key or key called promise? Open the door of despair and let God's pardon flood your soul, and you will be free.

Don't bite the bait. You can have triumph over temptation. But to do so, you must understand that there is a clear principle, and it's a common problem. It is a captivating process following a continual pattern, but praise God, you have a concrete promise and a constant provision.

Chapter Five

Intellectual Purity: Quenching the Fires of Fantasy

Today there is a battle that is going on for the minds of men and women, and it affects people of all ages. Sadly, many are falling in this battle because they have allowed their minds to become polluted by the influences at work in this world.

Recently, it was reported how pornography is present and prevalent. I quote, "Arizona lawmakers last week approved a resolution calling for efforts to prevent children from being exposed to pornography online, a move similar to those of legislated bodies in at least fifteen other states that are calling adult sexual content a public health crisis."

"It is an epidemic in our society, and this makes a statement that we have a problem," said Arizona state senator Sylvia Allen, a Republican whose chamber approved the resolution last Monday. She blamed pornography for contributing to a number of social issues, such as violence against women, sexual activity among teens, and unintended pregnancies. The Arizona legislation could possibly pave the way for future measures, such as blocking porn from the Internet at publicly-funded places like school and libraries.

Other resolutions have passed in Republican-controlled states like Montana and Tennessee. Utah was the first state to pass an anti-porn resolution in 2016. Another law in that state lets parents sue porn makers if their children need treatment for problems related to porn use.

One of the greatest struggles that exist today is this battle for purity of our minds. Solomon, the wisest man of his time said, "The thought of foolishness is sin." (Proverbs 24:9)

In the book of Genesis, we see God bringing the first judgment upon mankind. As He looked into the hearts of men and women in that day, this was what He saw: "Every imagination of the thoughts of his heart was only evil continually." (Genesis 6:5)

Today we must ask ourselves, how are we different from that generation? Is it not true that many men and women spend a great deal of time fantasizing about things that they desire to have or experience?

That we would struggle for the purity of our minds is nothing new. Notice what God says in Genesis 3:

> "Now the serpent was more subtil than any beast of the field which the Lord God had made. And he said unto the woman, Yea, hath God said, Ye shall not eat of every tree of the garden? And the woman said unto the serpent, We may eat of the fruit of the trees of the garden: But of the fruit of the tree which is in the midst of the garden, God hath said, Ye shall not eat of it, neither shall ye touch it, lest ye die. And the serpent said unto the woman, Ye shall not surely die. For God doth know that in the day ye eat thereof, then your eyes shall be opened, and ye shall be as gods, knowing good and evil. And when the woman saw that the tree was good for food, and that it was pleasant to the eyes, and a tree to be desired to make one wise, she took of the fruit thereof, and did eat, and gave also unto her husband with her; and he did eat. And the eyes of them both were opened, and they knew that they were naked; and they sewed fig leaves together, and made themselves aprons." (Genesis 3:1-7)

Here, we see the account of Eve as she comes face-to-face with the tempter and faces her own carnal desires.

***

The Screwtape Letters is a classic book of Christian fiction written by C. S. Lewis. The story is a series of letters between Screwtape and his nephew Wormwood, both of whom are demons. Throughout the story, the senior fiend advises his young apprentice on leading humanity astray, and he states, "The real use of the infernal Venus (Lewis's character whose focus is purely upon physical beauty and attraction) is, no doubt, as a prostitute or mistress. But if your man is a Christian and if he has been well trained in the nonsense about irresistible and all-excusing 'Love,' he can often be induced to marry her."

C. S. Lewis skillfully shows the dangers that exist in the area of fantasy or imagining, and he concludes that even a Christian is vulnerable in the area of temptation if he has given his mind over to the fires of fantasy.

About this very subject, Solomon wrote, "Can a man take fire in his bosom, and his clothes not be burned?" (Proverbs 6:27)

This is an amazing rhetorical question, and obviously, we see that no one could escape being burned if they embraced fire. Yet many a believer struggles to keep his thoughts pure as the fires of fantasy burn brightly. If we would be honest, we would admit that this battle in the area of pornography, the Internet, and videos affect many in the church today. Sadly, many excuse this sin by saying that it is not really a big deal because "everyone is doing it."

Erwin Lutzer, writing about the twelve myths Americans believe, wrote this: "Even before the Attorney General's report, a government study had found evidence that pornography can lead to crime. The minority report of the 1971 President's Commission on Obscenity and Pornography cited twenty-six cases drawn from all over the country in which immersion in pornography immediately preceded serious sex crimes, many of which were admitted by the perpetrators to be an enactment of pornography that was absorbed shortly before. For example: seven Oklahoma teenage male youths gang-attacked a fifteen-year-old female from Texas raping her and forcing her to commit unnatural acts with them. Four of the youths admitted to being incited to commit the act by reading obscene magazines and looking at lewd photographs." [1]

The need to quench the fires of fantasy is not new; it started in the Garden of Eden. What happened with Eve has continued throughout the ages since and is a recognizable pattern. Before Eve was ever attracted to the tree, she was attracted to the tempter. Before she was ever attracted to the fruit, she was attracted to the foe. We must not forget the subtlety of the evil one.

"Now the serpent was more subtil than any beast of the field . . ." (Genesis 3:1a).

As Satan came to Eve, he did not come as a slimy despicable creature crawling on his belly toward her, but rather, he came to her as a being of beauty. Before the fall, Satan was very attractive. One of the names given to Satan is Lucifer, which means "bright one." In Isaiah 14:12, we see him as that bright one. In Ezekiel 28, Satan is described as beautiful, the sum of perfection. Beauty is a wonderful thing if used in a right way, but Satan knows how powerful the attraction of beauty is, and he tries to use it for man's downfall.

In the New Testament, the apostle Paul warned, "And no marvel; for Satan himself is transformed into an angel of lig*ht." (2 Corinthians 11:4)

Putting Out the Fires of Fantasy

A. The attractions of life

The garden was a beautiful setting; perfection was all around. And there, Eve was attracted to the serpent. As she talked with the tempter, her heart was drawn toward that which God had forbidden. We see in Genesis 3:6, "And when the woman saw that the tree was good for food, and that it was pleasant to the eyes, and a tree to be desired to make one wise, she took of the fruit thereof, and did eat, and gave also unto her husband with her; and he did eat."

When Eve first saw the fruit, there was an attraction. We must note that attraction is a part of life every individual must deal with sooner or later. It is not the problem, but rather, how we handle the attraction makes all the difference in our lives.

Truly, the fruit was appealing, and it captivated her eyes and enslaved her heart. Eve was not the only one who faced this problem. Tragically, we see many examples in Scriptures of men and women enslaved by the attractions of life.

In Judges 14, we have the example of Samson: "And Samson went down to Timnath, and saw a woman in Timnath of the daughters of the Philistines. And he came up, and told his father and his mother, and said, I have seen a woman in Timnath of the daughters of the Philistines: now therefore get her for me to wife." (Judges 14:1-2)

Samson was a mighty man of great valor and courage and also an attractive person. Yet when he saw a woman in Timnath, he demanded to have her. Notice the reaction of his parents: "Then his father and his mother said unto him, Is there never a woman among the daughters of thy brethren, or among all my people, that thou goest to take a wife of the uncircumcised Philistines? And Samson said unto his father, Get her for me; for she pleaseth me well." (Judges 14:3)

Samson's parents could not understand why he had to go to the Philistines to find a wife. They could not understand why he had to get his wife from among pagans. Clearly, she was not the one for him, yet Samson's response was emphatic: "Get her for me; for she pleaseth me well."

The attractions of life, beauty, and sensuality were too much for Samson, and he paid the consequences for being enslaved by them.

Another example of someone trapped by the attractions of life was David, the great king of Israel. We read part of his sad story in 2 Samuel: "And it came to pass in an eveningtide, that David arose from off his bed, and walked upon the roof of the king's house: and from the roof he saw a woman washing herself; and the woman was very beautiful to look upon. And David sent and enquired after the woman. And one said, Is not this Bathsheba, the daughter of Eliam, the wife of Uriah the Hittite? And David sent messengers, and took her; and she came in unto him, and he lay with her; for she was purified from her uncleanness: and she returned unto her house." (2 Samuel 11:2-4)

Bathsheba was very beautiful to look upon. In response to seeing her, David became attracted, and then he inquired about her. His attraction became a trap, and his life was tainted by his poor response to it. Yes, Bathsheba was beautiful to look upon, yet her beauty was not the sin; it was David's dwelling on her beauty and fanaticizing in his heart that gave birth to a series of sins. This is what happens when we fail to guard our hearts.

Solomon put it this way: "Lust not after her beauty in thine heart; neither let her take thee with her eyelids. For by means of a whorish woman a man is brought to a piece of bread: and the adultress will hunt for the precious life." (Proverbs 6:25-26)

What a tragedy when a man allows himself to be captivated by attractions and this becomes a destructive force in his life. In the garden, Eve looked upon a fascinating and beautiful creature, and she started to fanaticize. Samson saw a woman and fanaticized and became a slave. David did not guard his eyes and heart and brought shame upon himself and his God.

There are a lot of beautiful attractions in this world. The sin is not in the attraction but rather what we allow to happen as a result of those attractions. When we do not control the attractions of life and guard our hearts, the fires of fantasy start to burn.

About the attractions of life, Jesus said, "Ye have heard that it was said by them of old time, Thou shalt not commit adultery: But I say unto you, That whosoever looketh on a woman to lust after her hath committed adultery with her already in his heart. And if thy right eye offend thee, pluck it out, and cast it from thee: for it is profitable for thee that one of thy members should perish, and not that thy whole body should be cast into hell." (Matthew 5:27-29)

Through these penetrating words, Jesus instructs us that we should do all we can to avoid being trapped by the attractions of life.

Eve, when she was attracted by the subtility of the serpent, did not turn from the attraction, but rather, she contemplated his lies—"Hath God said . . . ye shall be as gods"—and she fell victim to his deceit.

Intellectual purity can only occur when we first know how to handle the attraction of life instead of being handled by them.

B. The Appetites of Life

As we further consider Eve, we see that not only did she find the forbidden fruit to be attractive, but also, we are told "it was good for food." (Genesis 3:6)

Is there anything wrong with food? No. Is it bad to have an appetite? No. Without an appetite, we would die. However, we also see that with an uncontrolled appetite, we will die. This is true physically, but it is also true mentally and spiritually.

Eve rightly saw that the fruit was good for food, but the problem was that God had clearly told her that she was not to eat of it. She was trapped by her attraction as she focused upon her appetite and ignored the command of God.

In Matthew 4, as Jesus was tested in the wilderness, He became hungry. He had an appetite, and it was not wrong to be hungry. However, had He responded to Satan's temptation and used His power to satisfy that hunger, this would have been sin because His appetite would have been satisfied outside of the will of God.

Satisfying an appetite is not sin, but satisfying an appetite out of the will of God *is*. Either we control our appetites or they will control us.

David had this very struggle in view when he wrote these words in Psalm 119:9, 11: "Wherewithal shall a young man cleanse his way? by taking heed thereto according to thy word . . . Thy word have I hid in mine heart, that I might not sin against thee."

If we are going to stand against the appetites of life, we will have to develop an appetite, that is greater for the things of God, an appetite for holiness, an appetite for God's Word, and an appetite to know God and feed upon Him.

Today the world is littered with Christians who will not control their appetites and, as a result, have ruined their lives and testimonies. Remember, an appetite in and of itself is not wrong, but to satisfy it outside of the will of God is sin; and it is devastating.

The key to avoiding this trap is to develop an appetite for God and His Word that is greater than the impulse of sin.

D. L. Moody said it like this, "Either sin will keep you from the Book, or the Book will keep you from sin."

As we consider the appetites of life, the question comes down to what we are feeding our minds. If you feed upon the filth of pornography or sexually explicit entertainment, then, as a consequence, you will eat of the forbidden fruit and fall under the judgment of God.

C. The Attitudes of Life

Eve saw the fruit, and it was attractive. She also knew that it would be good for food, but more than this, she believed Satan's lie that it would make her wise.

> "And when the woman saw that the tree was good for food, and that it was pleasant to the eyes, and a tree to be desired to make one wise, she took of the fruit thereof, and did eat, and gave also unto her husband with her; and he did eat." (Genesis 3:6)

Eve believed that if she took that which God had prohibited, she would become wise; she could be like God; she could do her own thing.

This same attitude, "I can handle this," affects many people's lives today. Many approach the Internet thinking they can look and not be controlled. Their attitude is "I am wise, I can do my own thing, I have my rights."

The truth of the matter is that your attitude will determine your altitude. If you want to fly high for God, then your attitude must be one of utter dependence and obedience to God and His Word.

In the account in Matthew 4, Satan tried to get Jesus to take a shortcut to reign over the kingdoms of the world. He said to the Lord, "All these things will I give thee, if thou wilt fall down and worship me." (Matthew 4:9)

Did He have right to reign? Yes! But He would not get there through Satan but rather by obedience to the will of His Heavenly Father. The danger of a wrong attitude will often surface when we feel we have earned a right to indulge ourselves.

***

In 1986, Len Bias was the first-round draft pick of the Boston Celtics. Lefty Driesell, his former coach at the University of Maryland, called Bias the greatest basketball player that ever played in the Atlantic Coast Conference. However, less than forty-eight hours after he left for Boston, Len Bias died of cardiac arrest brought on by using cocaine. Len had been warned by a friend of the dangers but shrugged off the warning, thinking he had earned the right to indulge himself.

It is impossible to quench the fires of fantasy without maintaining a proper attitude of humble dependence upon God.

D. The Associations of Life

Why did Eve associate with the serpent? Why did she not just run when the serpent spoke to her? Eve was curious, and as the serpent spoke to her, she began to carry on a conversation instead of fleeing from this unusual being.

What about David? Why did he not leave the roof and remove himself from the situation? Why did he linger to look at Bathsheba?

The modern version of this might take place today in a chat room, that which begins innocently enough goes too far, and before long, the line is crossed, and the chat room leads to the bedroom.

The tragedy is that when we allow ourselves to be taken in by wrong associations. Before long, we end up adopting their value system.

Maybe this has happened to you, and you feel trapped. I have good news for you: The way out is to confess and abandon your sin.

> "He that covereth his sins shall not prosper: but whoso confesseth and forsaketh them shall have mercy." (Proverbs 28:13)

Now choose good and godly friends who can hold you accountable to a biblical value system.

Solomon, in the book of Proverbs, wrote, "He that walketh with wise men shall be wise: but a companion of fools shall be destroyed." (Proverbs 13:20)

We need to examine those with whom we associate ourselves in public, and then we must also examine what we do in private: videos, television, the Internet. If we associate with the foolish, the fires of fantasy will burn brighter, and we will end up getting hurt in the process and damaging the testimony of the Lord.

Life Lessons

As we look back on the example of Eve, what lessons can we learn that will help us quench the fires of fantasy in our own lives?

1. God is good and can be trusted.

The attack of the evil one in Genesis 3 was an attack upon the character of God. Satan convinced Eve that God was keeping something good from her; that if she ate the fruit, she would be freed from the authority of God and would be able to do whatever she wanted.

Note the following from David Breese's book *Satan's Ten Most Believable Lies*: "What a clever ploy! The enemy suggests that God is a moral tyrant, so bluenosed that He has forbidden His creatures any enjoyment whatsoever. The implication is that God filled the Garden with a delightful array of delicious fruit to taunt man, forbidding him to eat any of these fruits. God is, therefore, a negativist who made man merely to frustrate him. He is a cosmic sadist, inflicting an impossible set of rules and punishments upon man. God is, therefore, impossible to please, a total tyrant, so the best thing to do is to chuck the whole thing as of right now."[2]

We must learn that God is not a sadist, and He has given us all that we need to be fulfilled in life.

2. God's commandments were never given to hurt me but to help me.

When God told Adam and Eve not to eat from that tree, it was not to hurt them but to help them. When the principles of Scripture guide us away from the filth on the Internet, it is not to deprive us but to protect us. When God instructs us not to indulge in immoral thinking, it is not to hamper us but to make us holy.

> "He is the Rock, his work is perfect: for all his ways are judgment: a God of truth and without iniquity, just and right is he." (Deuteronomy 32:4)

3. Satan always appears in an attractive form.

He is a marketing specialist, and he knows how to disguise his evil intentions. He always uses young, beautiful, attractive people in the media to lure us to bite the bait. So be prepared!

4. I cannot trust my own heart.

> "The heart is deceitful above all things, and desperately wicked: who can know it?" (Jeremiah 17:9)

Because of this great truth, start your day in the Word of God. Be constantly memorizing and meditating on the glories of His Word and not the garbage of this world.

5. Fantasies lead to nightmares.

If we let those fires burn, we will be living our worst fears. It is very important to have an accountability partner who can ask us at any time the hard questions of life. This should be a good Christian friend of the same sex, if not married, and if one is married, it should be with their mate.

6. It is better to live in the realities of the day than to indulge in the dreams of the night.

Paul told young Timothy, "Flee also youthful lust." To us, he might say, "Be careful what you watch, and don't subject your eyes and hearts to internet sites that are lewd or pornographic."

For us, it may be wise to have a friend who can hold us accountable for our computer usage.

Intellectual purity – Yes, God wants us to quench the fires of fantasy, and we can do so by handling the attractions of life, the attitudes of life, and the associations of life, through the power of the indwelling Spirit and the Word of God.

My prayer is that God would help each one of us live victoriously in this area of intellectual purity as we apply these lessons from the first recorded sin of mankind.

Chapter Six

Why Not: Using Biblical Principles to Make Godly Choices

One of the questions that all Christians must face is, how to live a godly life in the midst of a generation given over to immorality and sensuality? It is amazing how many Christians are more concerned about what they can't do than about exploring what God's Word says in relation to Christian living. What we are really facing is the question of standards or Christian values.

There are many Christians in the twentieth century who sometimes feel as if they have settled in Sodom. A culture that once was dominated by Christian values is now one of the greatest spiritual challenges for American Christians. Once decency and order seemed to characterize the lives of individuals and communities. The institutions they created and the traditions they respected seemed to make American culture more hospitable to Christianity than any other culture in history. American society was regarded as a "Christian Society."

Early generations of Christians were concerned about "worldliness," and whatever that meant, it was seen as an aberration in American culture, not as essence. But today many Christians regard their culture itself as an implacable enemy, a constant threat to their own sanctity and to the stability of their families.[1]

In the face of such questions, some just go by a list of dos and don'ts. Nevertheless, in an ever-changing culture, our approach should be to establish biblical, immutable principles that apply to every culture and generation. But the problem goes beyond the activity to the heart of the problem which is attitudes. Truly the heart of the problem is the problem of the heart.

The Bible, in Titus 2:11, 12, states, "For the grace of God that bringeth salvation hath appeared to all men, teaching us that, denying ungodliness and worldly lusts, we should live soberly, righteously, and godly, in this present world."

To fully grasp the teaching of this text, we need to look at two key words. First is the word "teaching." In Greek, "paideuo" speaks of a child under development through strict training. It is to train up a child so they mature and realize their full development. Doing this requires administering necessary discipline. From this word, we get our English terms "pedagogue" or "pedagogy." This tells me that God's grace is a great pedagogue to bring me to maturity. It is not the soft, fluffy concept that a lot of Antinomians promote.

The next word is "world" or, better yet, "age." This is the word, "aion." R. C. Trench states they speak of "all that floating mass of thoughts, opinions, maxims, speculations, hopes, impulses, aims, aspirations, at any time current in the world . . . being the immoral atmosphere which at every moment of our lives we inhale, again, inevitably to exhale the subtle spirit of the world of men who are living alienated and apart from God."[2]

Thus, at present, only God's grace, our pedagogue, can help us set the disciplines and guidelines to answer the question "Why not?"

In this verse, we are reminded that the Christian life is a life that begins and continues in and through the grace of God. It is the grace of God that teaches us how to live in the midst of this present world or age.

In this brief study, we want to present seven principles that will teach us how to please God with our choices and conduct in this evil generation. More than just a list of things we can and cannot do, these principles will give us the biblical foundation by which we can judge any situation in life to determine if it is conduct appropriate for the child of God.

Purchased Possession

> "What? know ye not that your body is the temple of
> the Holy Ghost which is in you, which ye have of God,
> and ye are not your own? For ye are bought with a price:
> therefore glorify God in your body, and in your spirit,
> which are God's." (1 Corinthians 6:19-20)

The previous verses remind us that at present, we live in a body, and this body is the temple of the Holy Spirit of God. What is even more important for the believer to see is that his body is not his own to use or abuse as he sees fit. We have been bought with a price, and therefore our body belongs to the Lord. The passage that speaks of this great truth is found in 1 Peter 1:18-19: "Forasmuch as ye know that ye were not redeemed with corruptible things, as silver and gold, from your vain conversation received by tradition from your fathers; But with the precious blood of Christ, as of a lamb without blemish and without spot."

It is moving to think that we are a purchased possession of God and to consider the price the Lord paid to purchase our redemption.

The Greek term here brings the idea of loosening that which was bound, especially freeing those who are in prison. A synonym of this word "redeemed" is a word meaning "marketplace." This word also can have a prefix meaning "out." When put together, these form a beautiful word picture showing that we have been purchased out of the world's slave market and now belong to God. Also, we see the incredible price that God was willing to pay to make this purchase, the blood of His precious Son, Jesus Christ.

As we think upon how we should live in this present world, the first thing we must come to terms with is the fact that we are not our own— we are a purchased possession of the Living God. A good question for you to answer at this point is, "What value do you place on the price (the shed blood of Jesus Christ) that the Lord paid for your redemption?"

Peculiar People

As the English language continues to expand, words often take on new shades of meaning that they did not have before. Take for example the word "peculiar." Today this word means "odd." However, at the time the Bible was being translated into English, this word meant "unique" or "distinct." This is exactly what we see in 1 Peter, underscoring our unique position as the people of God.

The real concept of peculiar from the Greek text is a circle. We are encircled by God. That means we are very special and not part of anything out of the circle.

> "But ye are a chosen generation, a royal priesthood, a holy nation, a peculiar people; that ye should shew forth the praises of him who hath called you out of darkness into his marvellous light." (1 Peter 2:9)

The principle tells me that to live to please God in my generation, I must be distinct from the world, especially in my conduct. When people view the life of a Christian, they ought to be able to see that something is different to the glory of God.

Being different doesn't mean we are to be weird, but neither does it give me a license to be worldly. It means we are wonderfully special. Let's look at it this way: Because we are a peculiar people, we are His special people, and the world will know it because of how we live.

Having come to understand our unique position as the people of God, do our lives reflect the difference?

Partnership

A third principle that comes to mind, as we weigh what we should or should not do, as believers in Christ, is the principle of partnership.

In Romans 14, the apostle Paul was addressing the issue of doubtful things or what some might call gray areas. It was in that context that he made the following statement: "For none of us liveth to himself, and no man dieth to himself." (Romans 14:7)

In this verse, it is clear that, as a believer, we are in a partnership, we are connected, we are joined one to another within the body of Christ. This is very important as it relates to our conduct and choices in life. So I must take into account my brothers in Christ and never with my choices be a stumbling block.

Again, in Hebrews 10:24 we read, "And let us consider one another to provoke unto love and to good works."

Here, we are to "consider" or be mindful and to "provoke" or stir up one another. The "one another" statements of the Word of God are there to remind us that we are one body, and as such, we must be careful to live so as to edify and not tear down other members of Christ's body.

Many times I hear young people say, "This is my life, and what I do doesn't affect anyone else." This type of thinking is wrong and contrary to the Word of God. When I decide to go to a certain place or to participate in a certain activity, I must not only question how it will affect me, but also my brothers and sisters in Christ. It is the issue of not being a stumbling block (Romans 14:13).

We are on a great team in the body of Christ, and we should care about our teammates. We must ask ourselves, "Am I a help or a hindrance in their pursuit of God?" This is a very solemn question. Christians are in constant danger of being swept downstream by the currents of ungodly culture. They are prone to let the truth they know and the relationships they enjoy with God grow cold. They need to vigorously hold on to the immutable truth of Scripture.

This reminds me of the words of Robert Robinson who, in 1757, wrote, "O to grace, how great a debtor; daily I'm constrained to be! Let Thy goodness like a fetter bind my wondering heart to Thee. Prone to wonder Lord I feel it, Prone to leave the God I love; here's my heart, O take and seal it; seal it for Thy courts above."

Power

God not only saves and sanctifies by His power, but He also gives us His abundant power to serve Him. Isn't it wonderful to know that this gracious provision is sufficient for a godly Christian life? The Spirit of God made this so clear through the apostle Peter in 2 Peter 1:3, where we read, "According as his divine power hath given unto us all things that pertain unto life and godliness, through the knowledge of him that hath called us to glory and virtue."

In our evaluation of what we will and will not do, we must ask ourselves, will this lead to sin, causing me to lose my connection to God's power?

The psalmist wrote, "If I regard iniquity in my heart, the Lord will not hear me." (Psalm 66:18)

Sin in the life of a believer causes him to lose the power of God. As we establish our life values—those things we will embrace—this principle must be taken into account. Sin saps the life of power.

Peter wrote this concerning Lot, the nephew of Abraham: "And delivered just Lot, vexed with the filthy conversation of the wicked." (2 Peter 2:7)

Here, we see that as Lot was exposed day by day to the wicked lifestyles of the people of Sodom and Gomorrah, that exposure took its toll on his spiritual vitality.

As we decide our boundaries in the area of conduct, it is important to keep this in mind: Do you know that bad choices could rob you of your spiritual power?

In the previous verse, the word "vexed" is translated from a Greek word meaning "tortured" or "exhausted." Literally speaking, Lot's exposure to wickedness tortured and exhausted him spiritually.

As you make your choices in activities and amusements, you need to be honest with yourself. Do your choices leave you exhausted and torture your conscience before God? Also, it is interesting to note that the origin of our English word "amusement" is a word meaning "to not think."

Could it be that this is exactly what the devil has in mind? He wants to get us involved in activities that will cause us to shift our minds into neutral, no longer thinking or meditating about God.

God wants to give us life and power, but sin will rob us of that power. As we contemplate how to live a life pleasing to God and what our standards will be, the question we must keep in mind is this: Will it lead me to sin and, thus, rob me of God's power?

Production

On the night before the Lord Jesus went to the cross, He spoke with His disciples about how they should live after His ascension. A significant part of what the Lord communicated was His expectation that they should bear fruit.

> "Abide in me, and I in you. As the branch cannot bear fruit of itself, except it abide in the vine; no more can ye, except ye abide in me." (John 15:4)

Speaking of fruit-bearing in John 15, Jesus revealed that the key to being fruitful was abiding in Him. Abiding in Christ means that we will be involved in no activity that would dishonor Christ; we will make no choices that would not be His choices; we will make no plans that He would not approve; we will allow no diversion that displeases Him.

One question we must ask as we strive to live to please God and evaluate what we will allow ourselves to do is, will this activity or involvement limit my productivity for Christ?

What a tragedy that many Christians have become sterile because they have poisoned their system with worldly pleasures. We must remember the words of our Lord when He said, "Ye have not chosen me, but I have chosen you, and ordained you, that ye should go (literally, "move out") and bring forth fruit, and that your fruit should remain."

To not bear fruit is to sin against God and frustrate His purpose for saving us. Also, note that this verse goes on to say, "That whatsoever ye shall ask of the Father in my name, he may give it you." (John 15:16)

This means that if I do not bear fruit, my prayers will go unanswered. This would be a great place to pause and honestly ask yourself, am I bearing fruit in the work of God and seeing Him move in response to my prayers? What a pity to trade a life of fruitful service unto God for the empty rewards of gratifying our sinful desires.

Pleasure

The sixth principle we must observe as we strive to live to please God with our choices and conduct is the area of pleasure. The world in which we live puts a premium on pleasure just as the Word of God anticipated:

> "This know also, that in the last days perilous times shall come. For men shall be lovers of their own selves, covetous, boasters, proud, blasphemers, disobedient to parents, unthankful, unholy, without natural affection, trucebreakers, false accusers, incontinent, fierce, despisers of those that are good, traitors, heady, highminded, lovers of pleasures more than lovers of God." (2 Timothy 3:1-4)

Historians and newspaper columnist Max Lerner said, "We're living in a Babylonian society, perhaps more than Babylon itself . . . The emphasis in our society today is on the senses and the release of the sensual. All the old codes have been broken down."³

Make no mistake, sin does afford a measure of pleasure, but the world's pleasure is seasonal (temporary). Moses understood this principle, and it directed his choice as he turned his back on the riches of Egypt:

> "Choosing rather to suffer affliction with the people
> of God, than to enjoy the pleasures of sin for a season."
> (Hebrews 11:25)

The apostle Paul wrote about concerning pleasures out of his own personal experience. Take note of the words he used to describe the mindset of those who live to satisfy their desire for pleasures:

> "For we ourselves also were sometimes foolish, disobedient, deceived, serving divers lusts and pleasures, living in malice and envy, hateful, and hating one another." (Titus 3:3)

In contrast to the fleeting pleasures that the world can offer, the Word of God paints quite another picture for those who live to please God:

> "Thou wilt shew me the path of life: in thy presence
> is fulness of joy; at thy right hand there are pleasures for
> evermore." (Psalm 16:11)

And also,

> "They shall be abundantly satisfied with the fatness
> of thy house; and thou shalt make them drink of the
> river of thy pleasures." (Psalm 36:8)

In light of the pull of pleasures one must consider, will I live to please my flesh or God?" Both involve pleasures, but one is measured and fleeting, and the other is abundant and permanent. Which will you choose?

Paul wrote in 2 Corinthians 5:9 that it was his ambition to please the Lord. It almost seems contradictory that a holy man of God as Paul would say he was ambitious, yet that was the case because the word "labor" in the text is the word "ambitious." In Greek, the word for "accepted" means "well pleasing."

His driven desire of life, his ambition, was to live in a way to please his Lord.

Praise

The final principle to place in the balances is the practical matter of bringing praise to God.

Ephesians 1:6 states that a part of God's purpose in salvation is that we might bring Him praise, in light of His abundant grace:

> "To the praise of the glory of his grace, wherein he
> hath made us accepted in the beloved."

As we evaluate our standards and values, one important question we can ask is, will it bring praise to God? Or we might ask, will others praise God because I am involved in this activity?

Psalm 145:10 says, "All thy works shall praise thee, O LORD; and thy saints shall bless thee."

It is impossible to live and be involved in questionable things and yet be a blessing to God.

Our lives are to be an open book before the Lord and before fellow believers:

> "Neither is there any creature that is not manifest in
> his sight: but all things are naked and opened unto the
> eyes of him with whom we have to do." (Hebrews 4:13)

The fact that nothing is hidden from God should be a motivating factor that moves us to choose only those things that are clearly praiseworthy.

The apostle Paul told us that we are not even to think about things that are not worthy of praise:

> "Finally, brethren, whatsoever things are true,
> whatsoever things are honest, whatsoever things are just,
> whatsoever things are pure, whatsoever things are lovely,

whatsoever things are of good report; if there be any
virtue, and if there be any praise, think on these things."
(Philippians 4:8)

As he spoke to the church at Corinth, Paul told them that God's
glory and praise should be paramount in everything that they did.

"Whether therefore ye eat, or drink, or whatsoever
ye do, do all to the glory of God." (1 Corinthians 10:31)

Conclusion

When it comes to living the Christian life, often we want a checklist,
and some even go so far as to try to produce one.

- I will go this far and no further.
- I can look at this but not that.
- I can go here but not there.

Although there are certain things that should be on every believer's
list of dos and don'ts, the Christian life is far too dynamic to reduce to
just a checklist. This reminds me of the words of George MacDonald:
"Nothing is so deadening to the divine as a habitual dealing with the
outside of spiritual things." This was the main issue with the Pharisees in
the time of Jesus.

There are biblical principles by which you can measure the choices
of life and questions along the way. Mastery of these principles will give
you a biblical measure by which you can evaluate your attitudes and
actions. Remember, our lives should be governed not by the pleasures of
the world, but the principles of the Word of God.

Ask yourself these questions:

1. How will this activity help/hinder my spiritual life?
2. How will this activity protect/damage my body?
3. How will this activity help/hinder a fellow-believer who might
   follow my example?
4. How will this activity help/hinder my testimony to the unsaved
   world?

We should seek balance between strict legalism (obeying the letter of the law) and antinomianism (no respect for the law). Take the analogy of driving a car:

1. The legalist drives down the highway of life with his eyes glued to the speedometer, lest he go one mile over the speed limit.
2. The antinomian goes down the highway of life nervously, looking in the rearview mirror for the policeman.
3. The person motivated by God's grace in his life drives down the highway of life looking out the windows, enjoying the scenery because his daily walk with the Lord gives him the sense of what is pleasing to the Lord in anybody's) given situation.

In closing this chapter, the words of my good friend Dr. Charles Ryrie are fitting: "The question is not 'why not?' But 'why should I make that choice?'"

May God help you strive after the abundant life that can only come from living and walking in fellowship with the Living and True God.

Chapter Seven

Perfect or Forgiven: Can a Child of God Sin?

In the history of Christianity, there have been various views on the nature of a saved person's moral life while still living in this world.

Some have argued that regeneration (the born-again experience) is so transforming that immediately the newly saved sinner is no longer able to sin. Others agree in principle but indicate that the person must progress in holiness until they arrive at a state of sinless perfection; after which, they will no longer sin.

Others have noted that many people who seem to genuinely believe in Christ, nevertheless, struggle with their old habits. They note that salvation is "not by works" and, therefore, somewhat conclude that sin is not a major issue as it relates to the saved person's ongoing saved state. Such individuals are said to be backslidden and have been tripped up by their "old nature" or "sin nature" or "old man."

Still others have argued that man can "decide" to no longer follow Christ and, in so doing, can lose his salvation. Some preachers and evangelists are then hoping that this person will repent and get saved all over again.

What is the best understanding of this issue from Scripture?

We can safely reject the first and last opinions. Common sense would indicate that no human has ever achieved "sinless perfection." In fact, among those who claim "sinless perfection," they have developed an embarrassing "excuse" when someone obviously sins. They claim that it was not technically a "sin" but rather a "mistake." Unfortunately, some, laboring under the mistaken impression that they should be sinlessly perfect, develop depression and great guilt when they cannot match up to that high standard. The fact that many passages of Scripture challenge believers to godly living indicates that they are still capable of ungodly living.

On the opposite end, we can safely say that no child of God can be moved from the "saved state" to the "unsaved state." This conviction is based on several lines of argumentations:

1. By definition, salvation is a gracious work of God for us. We are saved by grace, and we stay saved by grace. If we can "stay saved" by works, then we are also "being saved by works."
2. Clear teachings of Scripture argue for the security of the believer. "My sheep hear my voice, and I know them, and they follow me: And I give unto them eternal life; and they shall never perish, neither shall any man pluck them out of my hand. My Father, which gave them me, is greater than all; and no man is able to pluck them out of my Father's hand. I and my Father are one." (John 10:27-30)
   "In whom ye also trusted, after that ye heard the word of truth, the Gospel of your salvation: in whom also after that ye believed, ye were sealed with that holy Spirit of promise, which is the earnest of our inheritance until the redemption of the purchased possession, unto the praise of his glory." (Ephesian 1:13-14)
3. The doctrine of the chastisement of the believer argues that God will "discipline" His children to keep them from falling away (if that were possible).
   "If ye endure chastening, God dealeth with you as with sons; for what son is he whom the father chasteneth not?" (Hebrews 12:7)
4. The doctrine of the discipline of the believer argues that God will at times take home a child of God if they persist in their sinful ways.

We see this truth in 1 John 5:16, where John speaks of a sin unto death. The Bible gives us examples of certain individuals who sinned unto death. Some examples which we see in Scripture are Nadab and Abihu, also Korah and those with him who rejected God's authority. In the New Testament, we see the example of Ananias and Sapphira, also certain ones in Corinth who partook of the table of the Lord in an unworthy manner.

> "For this cause many are weak and sickly among you, and many sleep." (1 Corinthians 11:30)

5. Certain terms used of saved individuals imply that the status is permanent.

    a. A "son" cannot become a "non-son."
    b. "Eternal life" must be "eternal."
    c. "Elect" cannot become "non-elect."

This leaves the middle position, but even here, there is controversy. Many theologians agree that man's final perfection is not realized until sinners receive their glorified bodies at the rapture or resurrection. However, they differ over the description of a saved person's current status.

One group takes a "stricter" view, arguing that saved individuals no long have "sin-natures" or the "old man." They argue that the "old man" was crucified with Christ and, therefore, is "dead" and unable to affect the sinner anymore. They acknowledge that a sinner may still sin, but they would insist that this be a rare event and that no child of God would ever slip back into a sinful lifestyle for any length of time. Therefore, they reject the concept of a "backslidden Christian."

I appreciate this view's desire to see all Christian living godly lives. However, the ends never justify the means. It is great to want the "end" of having all Christians living godly lives, but we can't alter the "means" by which the Word of God states that sinners become saints. The Bible indicates that both regeneration and sanctification are gracious works of God in the sinner's life. We can no more live victorious Christian lives over sin in our own energy than we can become born again by our good efforts. In fact, the Greek grammar of the verb in Ephesians 2:8 can be expanded to "For by grace you have been (past tense) and are being (present continuous) saved through faith."

Therefore, I conclude that there will be some Christians who fall into a backslidden state. The evaluation comes from God, not man, as to whether the person is truly saved. Some who never return may wind up demonstrating that they were never truly saved. They didn't "lose" their salvation; they never had it to begin with. Others will demonstrate God's gracious working in their lives by falling under conviction and repenting of their backward ways. The balance is to never overlook sin in a person's life, also not perverting salvation by faith and faith alone by overemphasizing a person's failures. "Although the sinful disposition will never hold the position of the master over the believer again, it continues with him the rest of his life and tries to exercise it's controlling power over him. Because it is so, the believer is confronted with a continuing conflict against the power of the sinful position."[1]

What does it mean to be a "new creature"?

Those offended by the concept that a true believer can be backslidden place some of their argument on the concept of the "new creature" that believers are in Christ.

> "Therefore if any man be in Christ, he is a new creature: old things are passed away; behold, all things are become new." (2 Corinthians 5:17)

They contend that if "all things are become new," then a believer shouldn't live according to his old way, and in fact, the "old man" or "old nature" no longer exists.

There are two conceptual problems with this argument; first is a time element, and the second is a metaphysical element.

As to the time element, we are all works in progress. The "all things are become new" statement has to work itself out in time. It is a legal evaluation, a "fact on paper," but the ramifications must be developed in the believer's life. We will not enjoy the perfection of that statement until we receive our glorified bodies in heaven. That is the background to the frequent observation that in the past, before I met Christ, I was "not able not to sin." Now in the present, having accepted Christ and been indwelt by His Holy Spirit, I am "able not to sin." In the future, when I am perfected in heaven, I will be "not able to sin."

A similar sequence is expressed under the topic of "sanctification." "Sanctification" comes from the same Hebrew and Greek words for "holy," "saint," and "set apart." We are currently "saints," positionally, in the legal sense of salvation. However, our "sainthood" is being worked out through our growth in practical sanctification. The goal is to make our practice match our position.

The second issue is metaphysical ("after the physical," referring to spiritual entities). In 1 Thessalonians 5:23, the metaphysical makeup of man is expressed: "And the very God of peace sanctify you wholly; and I pray God your whole spirit and soul and body be preserved blameless unto the coming of our Lord Jesus Christ."

Paul is saying that humans have a physical part (the body), and we also have immaterial parts (the soul or self-consciousness and the spirit or God-consciousness). These entities are the totality of what constitutes a human. Notice he does not include an "old man" or "new creature" because they are not metaphysical entities—they are not "things" that dwell in our body.

They simply represent our "old way of thinking" and our "new way of thinking." The "old nature" affected my body, soul, and spirit. My "new nature" affects my body, soul, and spirit. We are to encourage the new and ignore the old, but that does not mean that the "old" has been eradicated. And for that reason, we conclude that we can be "new creatures" who also are in danger of "behaving in the old ways."

Paul graphically describes his own struggles as a believer (present tense) with these two ways of thinking:

> "I find then a law, that, when I would do good, evil is present with me. For I delight in the law of God after the inward man: But I see another law in my members, warring against the law of my mind, and bringing me into captivity to the law of sin which is in my members. O wretched man that I am! who shall deliver me from the body of this death? I thank God through Jesus Christ our Lord. So then with the mind I myself serve the law of God; but with the flesh the law of sin." (Romans 7:21-25)

The amazing thing about this struggle is that Paul encourages his listeners to "reckon" themselves to be dead to the old ways. "Reckon" is an accounting term that means to "count" or "consider" something to be so.

"Likewise reckon ye also yourselves to be dead indeed unto sin." (Romans 6:11)

The point, however, is that we are not truly "dead" unto sin. We have been crucified with Christ, and therefore, we are able to legally and metaphorically "consider" ourselves to be dead (for it cannot be changed—we will realize this position some day in the future); but right now, we are not "dead" (as in "unconscious and unable to respond), and therefore, we must guard ourselves from falling into old sinful habits.

What does "dead" mean?

This brings up a crucial issue, the definition of "dead" in Scripture. "Dead" in Scripture does not mean "unconscious" necessarily. Those who reject Christ and are thrown into hell experience the "second death," but they are not unconscious. They are very much aware of what is happening to them. "Death," therefore, has the primary idea of "separation." In physical death, it is the separation of the body from the spirit. In spiritual death, it is the separation of the person from their Creator.

This understanding of "death" explains why one "dead to sin" can, nevertheless, sin for the time being. It also is helpful in understanding that as unsaved people, we are dead spiritually in that we are separated from God, but that does not mean that we are unconscious spiritually. Unsaved men can have spiritual thoughts and longings. It is the world, the flesh, and the devil that pervert those longings, but they still exist. And as God illuminates, guides, draws, and convicts, that "dead" sinner can eventually make the decision to receive Christ as Savior.

Chapter Eight

God, You Called: What Does the Call of God Mean for Me?

On a recent trip to Florida, I spent some time in the town of Lakeland, where I grew up. While there, I revisited many places that were important in my youth: the house where I grew up; the house of Mr. Don Kelso (the man who discipled me); the cemetery where my parents, grandparents, and my old basketball buddy Larry Bell are buried; and many other places that connected me to the past.

Each place brought back many memories; some good, some bad. Certain places reminded me of the life of sin that I had led prior to becoming a Christian. As I visited one of those places, an old song came to mind. The lyrics of that song are "Thanks to Calvary, I don't live here anymore." This song best expressed what was on my heart at that time. *Thanks to Calvary, I don't live anymore.* This truth especially gripped me when I drove past the house where I grew up. My memories from that house include many tragic family scenes.

As I reflected on all these things, I was reminded again of the grace of God and that He has a plan for every life. I went by the house the Kelso family lived in, and I thought back to the Bible studies Mr. Kelso held in his home when I was a teenager. There, I would spend hours studying and learning about God's Word.

I drove to my high school and stopped there and thought back about being in those halls. I remembered the number of kids who trusted Christ during those years. It was a wonderful time of reflection.

Looking back and remembering where you have been and where you are going is important, but one of the most important things you can remember is the call of God on your life. Maybe you're like I was, maybe your home situation was not good. Looking back, I can remember thinking, "God, it would be so wonderful to have a Christian home."

I was a kid who didn't know which way was up, yet through it all, God had a marvelous plan for my life.

In this brief study, we want to focus on the specific plan God has for each of His children. That plan, to say it another way, is God's call on your life.

The apostle Paul, in his letter to the Galatians, said that his call was from his mother's womb (Galatians 1:15). We must come to understand that God's call is not on part of our life but on all of it. How wonderful to know that a sovereign God is at work in our lives even before our salvation.

As we consider the call of God—what it is and how it comes about, I want to make reference to what God did in the life of Moses as seen in the book of Exodus. As we begin to read in Exodus 3, it is evident that God's call was upon the life of Moses:

> "Now Moses kept the flock of Jethro his father in law, the priest of Midian: and he led the flock to the backside of the desert, and came to the mountain of God, even to Horeb. And the angel of the Lord appeared unto him in a flame of fire out of the midst of a bush: and he looked, and, behold, the bush burned with fire, and the bush was not consumed. And Moses said, I will now turn aside, and see this great sight, why the bush is not burnt. And when the Lord saw that he turned aside to see, God called unto him out of the midst of the bush, and said, Moses, Moses. And he said, Here am I. And he said, Draw not nigh hither: put off thy shoes from off thy feet, for the place whereon thou standest is holy ground. Moreover he said, I am the God of thy father, the God of Abraham, the God of Isaac, and the God of Jacob. And Moses hid his face; for he was afraid to look upon God . . . And Moses answered and said, But, behold, they will not believe me, nor hearken unto my voice: for they will say, The Lord hath not appeared unto thee. And the Lord said unto him, What is that in thine hand? And he said, A rod. And he said, Cast it on the ground.

And he cast it on the ground, and it became a serpent; and Moses fled from before it. And the Lord said unto Moses, Put forth thine hand, and take it by the tail. And he put forth his hand, and caught it, and it became a rod in his hand." (Exodus 3:1-6, 4:1-4)

By looking at the working of God in the life of Moses, we see patterns that we can apply to our lives as we seek to understand the marvelous, majestic call of God on our own lives.

Personal Call

First, we see that this was a personal call. God said, "Moses, Moses." Have you ever considered that God knows your name? You may be one in a billion, but God still knows your name. "Moses, Moses." Just put your name there. God's call is personal; it is His personal call on your life.

Do you remember Jeremiah? When God called him, He indicated that He had a plan in mind specifically for him even before he was born (Jeremiah 1:5). As Jeremiah grew in his mother's womb, God had already set him apart for service. Then there is Saul (who later became the apostle Paul). When Jesus appeared to Saul on the road to Damascus, he too was called by name. These are just a few, but the Bible is filled with many examples of God's personal call on the lives of His servants.

How truly special it is to hear someone you love call you by your name. Isn't it incredible to consider that God calls us personally—by our name?

Private Call

As a teenager, I spent my summers on Word of Life Island, first as a camper and then later as a part of the camp staff. Often, throughout the summer, I would find time to get alone with God. During those times, I would find a quiet place where I could sit on a large rock overlooking the lake. It was during those occasions, in the privacy of my time with God, that it became very clear that God was calling me to His service.

May I ask, how is your private time with God? Do you sit still long enough, or are you alone long enough to hear the voice of God in your life? Busyness is no friend of intimacy with God. It has been said busyness can lead to bareness.

The privacy of the backside of the desert and of Mt. Horeb became God's megaphone for Moses. Was Moses alone in this type of experience? No, Paul spent a private time with God in the Arabian Desert. It was there that the apostle was instructed by God on the particulars of his mission, message, and the call of God on his life.

Purifying Call

The call of God is not only a personal call and a private call, but it is also a purifying call.

> "And he said, Draw not nigh hither: put off thy shoes
> from off thy feet, for the place whereon thou standest is
> holy ground." (Exodus 3:5)

Previously, we noted the words of the apostle Paul in Galatians 1:15: "God who separated me from my mother's womb . . ."

The call of God will separate you in a special way. It is purifying and will change your whole life because you will sense that God's hand is upon your life and that He has set you apart to do something unique for Him.

Isaiah's call was one that touched his lips and purified his soul:

> "Then said I, Woe is me! for I am undone; because I
> am a man of unclean lips, and I dwell in the midst of a
> people of unclean lips: for mine eyes have seen the King,
> the Lord of hosts." (Isaiah 6:5)

Knowing that God has marked you out for a specific work has a way of purifying your life. It will purify your thoughts, words, and deeds; and you will know that you can never be the same.

Remember, "Thanks to Calvary, we don't live here anymore."

Particular Call

The Bible clearly teaches that God has a particular job designed just for you or, maybe we could say it like this, a task you were designed specifically to carry out. God's particular call is tailor-made for you. That's the reason the apostle Paul said that God separated him from his mother's womb. "Separated" means "to set apart" or "to mark out." God gave Moses all the characteristics, all the abilities, all the background that he would need to fulfill His will and lead the nation of Israel. God's call for Moses was tailor-made.

You are very, very special to God, and He has a very particular call for you. For us, one of our greatest challenges is to set aside our own will and say "God, what is your particular call for me?"

The apostle Paul was called to go to the Gentiles. When the Lord called him on the Damascus Road, Paul's answer was "Lord, what will you have me to do?" Although God's plan was very detailed, Paul did not see everything all at once. For him, following God was a day-by-day process of walking with God. I remind you that the great lesson here is not knowing all the details but rather being obedient to the God of the details.

Moses was called to go and free the children of Israel; and without a doubt, I was called to go to Argentina. God had a design; He had a plan for my life.

As a teenager, I started to pray about going to the mission field. I remember the day that George Theis, my first Bible Club leader, sat with a group of us on a Florida beach and told us that God had called him and his wife, Joan, to Brazil. There were many tears, and although what God was doing in their lives was not clear to all of us, God's call was very particular to George and Joan Theis.

Many years later, George wrote to me from Brazil and asked if I would join him in the work. Immediately, I went to see Jack Wyrtzen, the founder of Word of Life, and, with the letter in hand, said, "Jack, what do you think about this? Isn't it awesome?" Jack looked right at me and said, "That would be great if that's what God wants you to do. But why don't you pray about starting a work in another country for Word of Life?" I was twenty-two, not yet married, and this was beyond my wildest imagination. I went back to my room, fell on my face, and cried out to God, saying, "Lord, why me?" Then I realized that my unworthiness was God's opportunity to magnify Himself.

The call of God is a particular call, and you should never think that God's will is like a smorgasbord where you can pick and choose what you want. God's will is especially tailored for you. Praise the Lord!

Permanent Call

> "For the gifts and calling of God are without repentance." (Romans 11:29)

Paul wrote this to the church at Rome. When God calls you to Himself, He calls you to service, and it's a permanent call, one that you can't just turn your back on. God's call is not something about which you can say, "I'll do it for three years." It's a permanent call on your life.

Having said that, keep in mind that God might move you around on His great chessboard of service, but it's His hand moving you and not you or others moving yourself.

A. Responsibility

It's a permanent call, but how does all this come about? The first step would be responsibility. In Exodus 3, Moses was on the backside of the desert, tending sheep. He was responsible, and this was manifested through his care for the sheep that were entrusted to him. Do you know when responsibility starts? It starts right now, right where you are. If you are responsible in the small things, God can trust you with greater things.

With this in mind, I thought about my last two years of high school and how God gave me much a burning passion for all my classmates. Many of them, by God's grace, came to Christ during those years. Every day, as I entered my high school, I walked in believing that this place was God's mission field for me. Often the call of God comes one step at a time, but it starts with responsibility in the small things. Little becomes much when God is in it, but also, much is little if God is not in it.

B. Remember Moses

> "And the angel of the Lord appeared unto him."

God's will can be so apparent, and He will make it so clear that, if you are committed to doing His will, you will not be able to miss it. I will say it again: God's call will be so clear and so apparent that you will not be able to miss it.

"Moses, Moses." God appeared to him in the burning bush, and he knew that he had met with God. That's what all of us should desire, not a secondhand experience but (figuratively speaking) a face-to-face meeting with God. He is not just the God of your fathers. He is your God and will manifest Himself to you.

On the night before Jesus Christ went to the Cross, He said to His disciples, "He that hath my commandments, and keepeth them, he it is that loveth me." (John 14:21 a)

And then He said, "He that loveth me shall be loved of my Father, and I will love him, and will manifest myself to him." (John 14:21 b)

Did you know that God makes Himself known to those who are obedient to Him? You will know that God is so real that you will not mistake His call.

Today God's revelation is found in Scripture. These words of the Spirit of God, through the apostle Paul, to a young man named Timothy are so fitting:

> "All Scripture is given by inspiration of God, and is profitable for doctrine, for reproof, for correction, for instruction in righteousness: That the man of God may be perfect, thoroughly furnished unto all good works." (2 Timothy 3:16-17)

"Thoroughly furnished" is the concept of being "totally equipped." Just as Timothy was totally equipped through the Scriptures for God's service, so are we. Yes, the will of God is the Word of God, and the call of God is found in the commandments of God.

Saturate yourself with the concepts of God through the Bible, and the call of God will become clear to you. Through the Scriptures, you can learn God's mind, and then you will be able to see God's road map.

C. Reverence

"Put off thy shoes off thy feet." (Exodus 3:5a)

Have you ever seen someone awestricken? Once you have experienced reverence, you will realize you can't play around with God. As a young man, I came face-to-face with this truth on the trip home from camp on Word of Life Island. The group I was traveling with stopped in Orangeburg, South Carolina. There, along the side of the road, Mr. Don Kelso gave a Bible study from the letter to the Hebrews on the awesomeness of God. His eldest son, also named Don, attended the same high school as I did.

As Mr. Kelso spoke, I turned to his son Don and said, "We've got one more shot at our high school, and we better not blow it." I had learned something about reverence for God.

When God gives you something to accomplish, it is a serious matter. Reverence Him and His call.

D. Resources

As we are nearing the end of this brief study, in Exodus 4, Moses said, "How can I go?"

To which God responded, "What is that in thine hand?"

These are the same words I heard when I was ready to throw in the towel during the early days of establishing the ministry of Word of Life in Argentina. There, in Buenos Aires, I turned on the radio and heard Jack Wyrtzen preaching from this passage in Exodus. When God asked Moses what was in his hand, he replied, "I've got a rod." And God said, "That's enough."

Consider this. Whatever you have, if it is placed in the hands of God, it will always be sufficient to allow you to obey God's command and meet the needs of the people God has called you to serve.

When I heard Jack say, "What do you have in your hands?" I replied aloud, "God, I have a basketball and a Bible." It was then that I understood that if you are following the call of God, then you have everything you need to do the job. You might say, "Oh, it's just an old rod." But when God is working, you will have the resources you need to face any task and to do great things for His glory.

Isn't it wonderful to know that the same God who called Moses is still calling people today? Why don't you place all that He has given you into His hands and let Him use you to bring honor and glory to His name?

In a day of committees and chessboard direction by human "lords" who have forgotten about the vital importance of the call of God in the life of the believer, they never experience the joy of the personal call of God in their lives. I laugh as I remember the words of Warren Wiersbe, "A committee is a group of individuals, who independently can do nothing, and corporately decide nothing can be done."

I am glad when Paul was called by God to go to the Gentiles. With the Gospel of the grace of God, he did not have to wait for approval by the Jerusalem Council.

The call of Christ in the life of a believer is to take up the cross and follow Him. It is a blood-stained banner of the precious Lamb of God and brings a certain stigma before a secular humanistic world. Some time ago, I visited the tomb of the great hymn writer Issac Watts in Bunhill fields in England, who lived and ministered in the late 1600 and early 1700. He authored more than 750 Christian hymns, but the words of his hymn, "There is a fount filled with blood," grips my soul.

As we muse on the call of God, let these words penetrate your heart:

> E'er since by faith I saw the stream,
> Thy flowing wounds supply,
> Redeeming love has been my theme,
> And shall be till I die . . .

Chapter Nine

Finishing Well: How You Can Successfully Run Life's Race

Often people live their lives thinking only of the here and now without ever looking ahead to the end of their lives. It is as if we avoid considering our end for fear that thinking about it will bring it to pass. However, when we look to the pages of Scripture, we find that often we are instructed to consider our end that we might live better now. The apostle Paul, as he was sharing his heartbeat to the elders of Ephesus, said, "But none of these things move me, neither count I my life dear unto myself, so that I might finish my course with joy, and the ministry, which I have received of the Lord Jesus, to testify the Gospel of the grace of God." (Acts 20:24)

The apostle Paul was saying that his present life decisions were directed by his future goal of completing the course. As we consider his motivation, we see that there is an inherent danger in running the race, the danger of not finishing well.

In this brief study, I want to call your attention to the danger of not finishing well. The basis for this study will be the text found in Hebrews 12:12-17, where we read,

> "Wherefore lift up the hands which hang down, and the feeble knees; and make straight paths for your feet, lest that which is lame be turned out of the way; but let it rather be healed. Follow peace with all men, and holiness, without which no man shall see the Lord: Looking diligently lest any man fail of the grace of God;

lest any root of bitterness springing up trouble you, and thereby many be defiled; lest there be any fornicator, or profane person, as Esau, who for one morsel of meat sold his birthright. For ye know how that afterward, when he would have inherited the blessing, he was rejected: for he found no place of repentance, though he sought it carefully with tears."

As we consider the tremendous importance of moving out for God, we must be aware that there is a danger of not finishing the race. Let me be clear, right up front, that this has nothing to do with salvation and everything to do with fulfilling God's purpose for your life.

Here, in this passage, the writer to the Hebrews gives a very clear command when he wrote, "looking diligently" (v.15). The word behind this small phrase, "looking diligently," is the same word as "overseer" when translated in 1 Peter 5:2 and Acts 20:28. The Greek word is "episkopos," which means "looking over." It is the idea of checking something out, looking everything over, being an overseer. And so for us, the injunction is that we are to check out our lives. We are to take a good look around, knowing that if we don't, we might not finish well.

Thinking about this, it is as if God is saying that we should listen, look around, check things out, and make sure that everything is in place to finish well.

In the preceding verses of this same chapter (Hebrews 12), the author has already written concerning the race we are to run. As he describes this race, the word he uses is the word for a marathon, not just a hundred-yard dash; it's the word for a distance run. With this in mind, as we run life's marathon race, the tremendous challenge before us is not only just to run but also to run so as to cross the finish line.

As we consider finishing well, what are the things that can impede you and me from crossing that finish line? From this passage, I see four distinct challenges we must face if we are going to finish well.

Discouragement

In Hebrews 12:12, the writer says, "Wherefore lift up the hands which hang down, and the feeble knees."

Lift your hands. Lift those feeble knees. This is a vivid picture of one who is discouraged. But what causes discouragement? The word "wherefore" points us back in the passage to the previous verses that speak of God's discipline in the life of the believer. The Bible clearly teaches that every child of God is subject to chastisement, and that chastisement is God's discipline given that we might be partakers of His holiness.

Let me remind you that a life that really succeeds is a life that is marked by discipline. In the race of life, God will often bring us through times of discipline, challenges, hard times, or tests. And in the midst of God's discipline, some get discouraged. You may be reading this today, and the truth is that you've been running in this race, and you are discouraged. To you, God is saying, "Lift up those hands and those feeble knees."

Often runners get to place where there seems to be no more energy in reserve; they simply have nothing left, and their arms are hanging down, and their knees get weak. Through this passage, God is saying that as we're running life's marathon race, and we're going through the disciplines and the routines of life, don't get discouraged because discouragement will cause you to quit and not cross the finish line.

Let me make this very clear: All of us are prone to discouragement. There have been times when I have wanted to quit, times when I have said "Why take another step?" We all tend toward discouragement because we are flesh. It is at this time that God says, "Lift up your hands! Strengthen those feeble knees!" The whole picture is that of being reinvigorated.

In the midst of discouragement, in the midst of these disciplines of life, how do you lift your hands? How do you strengthen your feeble knees? You do it by patiently waiting on God and allowing discipline to run its full course and accomplish God's purpose. And this you do all while knowing that God loves you and that He has a plan for you and will keep that flame alive in you as long as you are walking in submission to Him. On the other hand, if we refuse to submit to God's discipline, then we open ourselves up for discouragement, which will cause us not to finish the course.

And as you think about that, ask yourself, "How can I recharge my tank?" I have found that if I do not daily meet with my Lord, in His Word, and get my spiritual batteries recharged, then I open myself up for discouragement. If we are faithful in this area, then we will understand that the disciplines of life are a part of God's plan to conform us to the image of Christ. Negligence, in this area alone, has caused many an individual to not finish well.

But what else could cause me not to finish well? Not only is there the potential for discouragement, but your life also can be sidelined by detours—the detours of life.

Detours

We read in Hebrews 12:13, "And make straight paths for your feet, lest that which is lame be turned out of the way; but let it rather be healed."

Make straight the path. In other words, don't veer off the course. Let me again remind you that this life is a marathon, and there are no shortcuts. One of the things that happens in many lives (especially young men and women) is that they want to take the easy way. They want to take a shortcut, but what they are really taking is a detour. We must remember that the devil is a specialist at presenting us with simple, attractive, easy detours that will cause us not to finish the course. At first, simple things that seem innocent come across your path, and if you are not wise, they can cause you to detour.

Sometimes this happens to a student's life. They try to take a shortcut but soon find the shortcut is really a dead end.

To young Timothy, Paul wrote, "Study to shew thyself approved unto God, a workman that needeth not to be ashamed, rightly dividing the word of truth." (2 Timothy 2:15)

The word translated as "study" is a word meaning "diligent or minute study," which requires work. Don't detour. Remember that the Scriptures say that there must be diligence. That also means dedication.

Again, Paul wrote, "And if a man also strive for masteries, yet is he not crowned, except he strive lawfully." (2 Timothy 2:5)

Here, Paul used the imagery of a runner competing in a race and said that the runner will not be "crowned" (Crowns were rewards given to those who successfully completed the race.) unless he obeyed the rules. One of the quickest ways to get disqualified in a race is to take a shortcut. So here again, we see that in the race of life, we must not take detours if we are to finish well.

Dislocation

Once again, in verse 13, we read, "And make straight paths for your feet, lest that which is lame be turned out of the way."

The idea here is that, as you're running the course, you must remove the obstacles from your path in order that you might not pull up lame.

Many athletes have had to drop out of the race because they hit an obstacle on the track that caused them to pull up lame. Often the smallest stone can cause a dislocation, which prevents the runner from crossing the finish line.

Stop and ask yourself, what type of obstacles are in the path of your life that might cause you to pull up lame? In the context of this passage in Hebrews, it was a lack of faith and trust in God, a lack of submission to God's work of discipline. To the Hebrews that were experiencing God's work of discipline, that work became a big obstacle. Let me offer you a word of caution: If you do not submit to the disciplines of God in your life, instead of them helping you along the way, they will transform your attitude into an obstacle that will get you off track.

This study is all about finishing the race, and again, it is important that we remember that this is not in reference to salvation, but rather, it is focusing on the idea of fulfilling all that God has planned and purposed for your life.

The apostle Paul said it like this, "Not as though I had already attained, either were already perfect: but I follow after, if that I may apprehend that for which also I am apprehended of Christ Jesus." (Philippians 3:12)

Paul recognized that God had planned specific things that He desired to complete in Paul's life, so his goal was to fulfill those very things that God had planned for him.

Defilement

A final danger found in this passage is the aspect of defilement that can come into one's life.

Hebrews 12:15 says, "Looking diligently lest any man fail of the grace of God."

Now this little word "fail" is a word meaning "to fall short, to be different." It's the idea of being left behind in a race or of failing to reach a goal. You can see the same concept in Hebrews 4:1: "Let us therefore fear, lest, a promise being left us of entering into his rest, any of you should seem to come short of it."

The same word is translated as "to come short of it." Again, the idea is not reaching the intended end.

Considering what the writer of Hebrews is saying, we see a warning against falling short of God's grace by becoming defiled. God's grace is His marvelous provision that we do not deserve. That provision is for salvation, and it also extends to our sanctification and our service. To say it another way, we're not only saved by grace, but we're also sanctified by grace, and by God's grace, we serve Him.

Looking closer at the danger of defilement, we see four areas in which defilement may come.

A. Attitude

One of the first places where we can become defiled is in our attitude. Often people say that it's only their actions that matter, but let us remember that our actions are really energized by our attitude. As your attitude is, so will your actions be. And here, the writer to the Hebrews is right on target concerning an attitude that can defile you. That attitude is called bitterness.

Notice his words from Hebrews 12:15: "Looking diligently lest any man fail of the grace of God; lest any root of bitterness springing up trouble you, and thereby many be defiled."

The idea of the root of bitterness is a bitter poisonous plant springing up ("germinating" is the word in Greek) to trouble, to crowd, or to annoy you and, if successful, defile you. I've known so many people who have had their whole lives destroyed by the root of bitterness.

How does someone come to the place where the root of bitterness germinates within them, sending its poison through their veins and defiling not only themselves but also others? It happens by not properly handling anger.

As human beings, we're not robots, and part of our individual makeup is our emotions. Our emotions are evident being seen through laughing, crying, loving, expressing anger, etc. With this in mind, some are confused by the text in Ephesians that says, "Be angry and sin not." There are certain things that should anger us: evil, wrong, injustice. As a result, anger over these things is proper. What this text is saying is that we are not to stew on our anger, but rather, we are to channel it properly. Handle the problem and then move on. Do not let our anger get out of control. If you are angered by what you believe to be justifiable but let your anger stew (letting the sun go down on your wrath), you are giving an opportunity to the devil, and bitterness will spring up. If there's a problem, handle it biblically. Go before the Lord, and make sure your attitude is right. Then go to the person, and get the problem resolved. Don't let it germinate and spread to everyone around you and, thereby, many be defiled.

So there is defilement that can occur in our attitude, and another form of defilement found in this passage can come through our appetites.

B. Appetites

In Hebrews 12:16, we read, "Lest there be any fornicator, or profane person, as Esau, who for one morsel of meat sold his birthright."

The writer says that Esau was a fornicator—what does he mean? Fornication is not necessarily saying that Esau had some perverse sexual relationship. The idea is this: Esau was a fornicator because he lived to sanctify his fleshly desires. The root of fornication is living to satisfy fleshly desires. Not all appetites are bad, but any appetite that is out of control will destroy you. And appetites not regulated by the Word of God will defile.

So as we consider the causes of defilement, first, we have seen attitudes, which are not properly channeled; then appetites, which are not properly controlled; but then we see also an accessibility to that which is not properly condoned.

C. Accessibility

This passage says that Esau was a "profane" person. The word translated to "profane" means "accessible." He left himself open to wrong influences. In our lives, we need to be open to God but closed to sin. Are you accessible? Are you an easy take for the evil one? If so, then chances are good that you will not finish the race.

D. Accounting

In looking at defilement, a final area to which we must focus our attention is the area of accounting. You see, Esau made an evaluation; he counted the cost before him and determined that the one morsel of meat was worth more than his birthright.

What's your value system like? As you add things up, where do you place value? As you look at life, be aware that there are pleasures and people that will try to lure you into sin. Do you know what God is saying? Add it up. Run the numbers. Put it on a balance sheet. You will find it is simply not worth it.

The tragedy of this text is that Esau "found no place for repentance." The passage says, "For ye know how that afterward, when he would have inherited the blessing, he was rejected: for he found no place of repentance, though he sought it carefully with tears."

Esau was "rejected"; he was disapproved. Avoiding disapproval was what motivated the apostle Paul as he wrote, "But I keep under my body, and bring it into subjection: lest that by any means, when I have preached to others, I myself should be a castaway." (1 Corinthians 9:27)

Paul disciplined his fleshly appetites that he might not find himself disapproved (castaway) and fail to finish well.

Sometimes it seems as though God unfairly restricts our opportunities for "fun" by the demands of discipleship. Years ago, veteran missionary evangelist G. D. Watson (1845-1924) explained his view of God's call on his life and how he wanted to finish well.

OTHERS MAY, YOU MAY NOT

> "If anyone wishes to come after Me, he must deny himself, and take up his cross and follow Me. For whoever wishes to save his life will lose it; but whoever loses his life for My sake will find it." (Matthew 16:24-25)

If God has called you to be truly like Jesus in all your spirit, He will draw you into a life of crucifixion and humility. He will put on you such demands of obedience that you will not be allowed to follow other Christians. In many ways, He seems to let other good people do things which He will not let you do.

Others who seem to be very religious and useful may push themselves, pull strings, and scheme to carry out their plans, but you cannot. If you attempt it, you will meet with such failure and rebuke from the Lord as to make you sorely penitent.

Others can brag about themselves, their work, their successes, their writings; but the Holy Spirit will not allow you to do any such thing. If you begin to do so, He will lead you into some deep mortification that will make you despise yourself and all your good works.

Others will be allowed to succeed in making great sums of money, or having a legacy left to them, or in having luxuries, but God may supply you only on a day-to-day basis because He wants you to have something far better than gold, a helpless dependence on Him and His unseen treasury.

The Lord may let others be honored and put forward while keeping you hidden in obscurity because He wants to produce some choice, fragrant fruit for His coming glory, which can only be produced in the shade.

God may let others be great but keep you small. He will let others do a work for Him and get the credit, but He will make you work and toil without knowing how much you are doing. Then to make your work still more precious, He will let others get the credit for the work which you have done; this is to teach you the message of the Cross, humility, and something of the value of being cloaked with His nature.

The Holy Spirit will put a strict watch on you and, with a jealous love, rebuke you for careless words and feelings or for wasting your time, which other Christians never seem distressed over. So make up your mind that God is an infinite sovereign and has a right to do as He pleases with His own and that He may not explain to you a thousand things which may puzzle your reason in His dealings with you.

God will take you at your word. If you absolutely sell yourself to be His slave, He will wrap you up in a jealous love and let other people say and do many things that you cannot. Settle it forever. You are to deal directly with the Holy Spirit. He is to have the privilege of controlling your tongue or chaining your hand or closing your eyes in ways which others are not dealt with. However, know this great secret of the kingdom: When you are so completely possessed with the Living God that you are, in your secret heart, pleased and delighted over this peculiar, personal, private, jealous guardianship and management of the Holy Spirit over your life, you will have found the vestibule of heaven, the high calling of God.[1]

Summing it up!

As we draw this study to a close, let us again consider the four challenges we must overcome if we will finish well.

Discouragement: Is there something out there today discouraging you? If so, get reinvigorated through the Word of God.

Detours: Are you off the path? Have you taken the devil's shortcut? Then get back on the path of righteousness.

Dislocation: Is your life out of joint because you have not removed something blocking the way and, therefore, your life and testimony are lame?

Defilement: Consider your *attitudes, appetites, accessibility,* and *accounting.* Each of these has the potential to defile your life, rendering you unfit or unable to complete the race God has set before you.

In all this, we need to understand that God wants us to finish well *and we can.*

God has provided everything we need to run our race to the end, but we'll never finish well if we do not keep our eyes on the course we are running. Let us purpose to keep our focus on the goal that we may stand before our Lord having finished our course well.

Chapter Ten

This Is Christian Music: Three Guiding Questions about Music

In this brief study, we will look at three questions that concern Christian music. What is the purpose of music? What are the pitfalls of music? And what are the principles for music?

Although this is not an exhaustive treatment of the subject, the goal of this study is to give the reader solid guidelines to make biblical choices about music.

Music plays an important part in life and can be used for good or bad. It is of utmost importance to honor God with our music. Charles Haddon Spurgeon said, "Our music should be as biblical as our message."

What Is the Purpose of Music?

From the Bible, we learn that when the foundation of earth was laid, music was there (Job 38:7). From the beginning, music has always been part of God's program. In this section, we will see various aspects of music but one overall biblical purpose—to glorify God.

A. Music Directs Our Worship to God

It is God's desire that our music direct our worship to Him. But what does it mean to worship God? A simple definition is to proclaim the worth of God. Given this definition, music is either used to declare the worth of God or to exalt the things of this world system.

Another aspect of worship is adoration. Adoration, simply put, means to bow or prostrate oneself. An example of adoration is found in Genesis 17:3. There, we see Abraham falling on his face before God. The point of adoration is to show honor.

Music should fulfill the purpose of proclaiming God's worth, causing one to adore Him. When we allow music to fulfill any purpose other than to glorify God, I believe we essentially turn our backs on God and honor the world's standards.

"The first musicians specifically set apart for God's praise seem to appear much later in 1 Chronicles 16, when David assigned the first official worship leaders in Israel to minister before the Ark of the Covenant. It is important to note that David chose Levites, who were sanctified or set apart to God's service. Leading worship to God in the Old Testament was not something allowed for just any musician, nor would they use just any music. Everything and everyone was carefully set apart, out of reverence and fear of the awesome Jehovah. Even though we are not under the law today, we find an important principle here for selecting the musicians and the music for use in a worship service."[1]

B. Music Proclaims God's Righteousness

Next, we see that music is a way to proclaim the righteousness of God. Psalm 145:7 says, "They shall abundantly utter the memory of thy great goodness, and shall sing of thy righteousness."

God uses music to show forth His person and His righteousness. Music that declares God's righteousness is different from any other type of music, and the unbelieving world can see that. Today much of so-called contemporary Christian music does not declare God's righteousness. Let me be crystal clear on this point: If music leaves out Jesus, if it leaves out the message of salvation and makes no mention of sin, then it is not of God. Regretfully, this type of music is geared toward gratifying the base nature of man and misses the purpose of bringing glory to God.

C. Music Announces the Messiah and Blesses His People

Music is not only for the purpose of directing our worship to God and for proclaiming His righteousness, but it is also to show forth the Messiah.

Speaking of the coming of the Messiah, Isaiah 35:6 says, "Then shall the lame man leap as an hart {dear} and the tongue of the dumb sing."

Music is to announce the Messiah, Jesus Christ Himself. How wonderful to think of music announcing Jesus as the Messiah. The majesty of a piece of music, such as Handel's "Messiah," is a blessed example of this truth.

These three aspects of the biblical purpose for music are not exhaustive but give a standard we can hold up for our music. At this point, some good questions to ask yourself might be: Does my music cause me to worship God? Does the music I listen to proclaim God's righteousness? Does my music help me tell a lost and dying world about Christ?

What Are the Pitfalls of Music?

A pitfall is a snare, a trap, a hidden danger. In this section, we want to address the hidden dangers of some Christian music that falls short of the biblical purpose presented in the previous section.

A. It Creates a Climate for Deception

When we say that music is Christian, we are saying it is about Christ. If our music is about Christ, then it should honor Him. The problem we are faced with today is that much of what is sold under the banner of Christian music has nothing to do with Christ. This is a deception, and many people are deceived. Sad to say, many parents have been deceived by their children. Often young people say, "I'm going to a Christian concert." In reality, some of these concerts differ very little from a secular rock concert. Is this Christian?

The "Medium" of Music

Consider the following testimony of drummer Mickey Hart regarding the mediumistic-musical method of Grateful Dead:

> I think of the musician's job as that of a psychopomp, someone who conducts spirits or souls to the other world . . . *Grateful Dead* was a ferryman, a conduit, a bridge to the spirit world, and the band provided a musical experience that offered safe passage to

the other side . . . Acoustic alchemy was necessary for the successful completion of the round trip.[1]

In his book, *Music, The Brain, and Ecstasy*, Robert Jourdain wrote of the mystical ecstasy that music can provide. He states,

> "Ecstasy melts the boundaries of our being . . . engulfs us in feelings that are 'oceanic.' A defining trait of ecstasy is its *immediacy* . . . Ecstasy happens to our*selves*. It is a momentary transformation of the knower . . . Music seems to be the most immediate of all the arts, and so the most ecstatic . . . Nonetheless, once we are engulfed in music, we must exert effort to resist its influence. *It really is as if some 'other' has entered not just our bodies, but our intentions, taking over.*"[2]

B. It Promotes a Degeneration of Values

No life degenerates in one step. There is a gradual digression or degeneration, compromising a little here and a little there until, in time, standards are eroded.

Jack Wyrtzen, the founder of Word of Life, used to say that this generation would be marked by two words: compromise and confusion. Jack wasn't a prophet, but those words have born true. If we are willing to compromise in the area of music, the question we must ask ourselves is, what's next?

Compromise destroys value systems. Many people who have been involved in tremendously destructive activities have saturated their minds with rock and heavy metal music, illustrating how music can destroy. Should we not steer a clear path around anything that resembles this type of music? Today many Christians are saturating their minds with extremes in Christian rock and are sadly unaware that it is eroding their value system. Our real battle is not with people around us but the passion within us. We must honestly ask, does the music I listen to promote fleshly passions in my soul?

A worldly church puts the emphasis on fun and entertainment to the expense of edification and evangelism.

C. It Damns the Sinner

When those who do not know Christ as Savior go to what is essentially a rock concert yet the concert is called Christian, they often come away thinking they have had an experience with God. But the truth is, if their exposure is not genuine, they remain separated from the life of God, which is found only in Jesus Christ. My question is this, have they not been deceived? If a concert is promoted as Christian but does not honor and point the way to Christ, then it deceives and is no less than a false gospel.

D. It Dishonors the Savior

As we conclude this section on the pitfalls of music, I want to tell you that much of contemporary Christian music dishonors the Savior. It's a slap in the face of God. The purchase price of our salvation was the very blood of Jesus Christ. Jesus came as a sacrifice, as a substitute, to take our place at Calvary. When He is not the central theme of Christian music or a so-called Christian concert, we cheapen His grace and we dishonor His person.

Years ago, as a nineteen-year-old on Word of Life Island, I wrote this poem:

> "Oh take me back to the old rugged cross which felt the
> flow of His crimson blood. The praise of men and worldly
> glitter will never soothe my pain or break my fetters. Smooth,
> smooth never shall it be for the place was called Calvary."

You see, it's still an old rugged cross. It's not smooth. It's not glittering. It's not shining. It's not applauded by the world. As a matter of fact, the world doesn't like the cross. Until they come to Christ and are transformed by His grace, God's music will not be their music.

If Christ is not the central theme of all we do, then we dishonor Him.

What Are the Principles for Music?

We will conclude this study by looking at this final question, a most important one, because everything we do as a Christian ought to find its basis in biblical principles.

Today we are facing a blight on the church. This blight exists because much of our agenda is geared toward pleasing man, not glorifying God. As we evaluate our music, the question we must ask is, who is being served, man or God? If we would live to please God, we must not only be driven by His purpose while avoiding the pitfalls, but we must also be guided by His principles. What are these guiding principles?

A. Music Should Glorify God

It says in 1 Corinthians 10:31, "Whether therefore ye eat, or drink, or whatsoever ye do, do all to the glory of God."

Christian music, like everything else in our lives, should bring glory to God. How much of today's music glorifies God? If the words being sung say little or nothing about God, can it really glorify God? If we are honest, we would have to say that it doesn't. The truth is that it glorifies the flesh and mimics the world.

Have we drifted? Have we turned our backs on what God really intended music to be in the life of the Christian?

B. Music Should Be Grounded in Truth

In Ephesians 5:19, immediately following the command to be filled with the Spirit, the Bible teaches us that one of the manifestations of a Spirit-filled person is singing: "Speaking to yourselves in psalms and hymns and spiritual songs, singing and making melody in your heart to the Lord."

What a tremendous statement! We see from this passage that someone who is Spirit-filled will be one who makes and listens to music—music that is thoroughly biblical. This type of music is found in psalms, hymns, and spiritual songs. The first two types, psalms and hymns, are familiar to us. Psalms are those portions of Old Testament Scripture recorded in the book of Psalms, which were originally songs of praise and worship dedicated wholly unto God. Hymns are those cherished songs that have been a part of the worship of the church since the earliest days. Hymns are songs that express the truths of God's Word but are not taken from the book of Psalms. The third type of music, spiritual songs, though less familiar to us, is no less clear in meaning. This type of song carries a spiritual theme or communicates a spiritual truth. Because each of these has its basis in Scripture, each is grounded in biblical truth.

C. Music Should Produce Godliness

In 1 Corinthians 10:23, we read, "All things are lawful for me, but all things are not expedient: all things are lawful for me, but all things edify not."

To edify is to build up. Good Christian music builds up. As you evaluate your music, you should ask, does it edify, does it build up, or does it tear down? Does it erode biblical values and godly virtues? Music should be a tool to encourage the development of Christian character, not a source of temptation to adopt the conduct of the world.

Through the years, I have had the incredible privilege of seeing thousands of young people reached with the Gospel and their lives transformed by the grace of God. Yet as we share the wonderful Word of God with teenagers around the world, we have never found compromise in the area of music to be necessary. Jack Wyrtzen used to say, "What we want is happy music—music that leads to a holy manner of life. When we have that, kids will love it, and Christ will be glorified!"

D. Music Should Be without Guile

Music should be without guile, not causing the believer to stumble:

> "But take heed lest by any means this liberty of yours become a stumbling block to them that are weak." (1 Corinthians 8:9)

This portion of Scripture speaks about doubtful things or things that might offend. Here, Paul says that he would not do anything that might offend or be a stumbling block. Today much of contemporary Christian music is very offensive to some and even is a stumbling block to others. For a Christian to persist in questionable music without regard for the brethren is clearly wrong, and it is sin.

How many Christian kids, those who long to embrace the world's music, find their base desires satisfied as they give in to this type of doubtful music? It becomes a stumbling block to them and others around them. It is sad to see how something that God meant for good, when it is used in the wrong way, can cause some to stumble.

What we denounced years ago and burned at campfires—records, then cassettes, and even CDs—is now being brought into the home and church as an accepted and even preferred means of worship. We live in a day when multitudes flock to so-called Christian concerts and music festivals. There, Christian artists are seen as stars (some even like rock stars) and not servants whose only desire is to glorify Christ. My questions are these: Is it a stumbling block? Does it glorify God? Does it edify?

In 1 Thessalonians 5:22, we read, "Abstain from all appearance of evil."

Browse the covers of much of the contemporary Christian music being produced today, and you will find very little difference between these and the covers of any secular band.

We are told in Scripture that we should abstain from all appearance of evil. When music is without guile, it will have no appearance of evil:

> "That ye may be blameless and harmless, the sons of God, without rebuke, in the midst of a crooked and perverse nation, among whom ye shine as lights in the world." (Philippians 2:15)

E. Music Should Not Be for Personal Gain

The final principle we will look at relates to the motivation behind the music. Much of the ministry of proclaiming the Gospel throughout the years has been enhanced by means of good Christian music. Countless Spirit-filled musicians have been used by God to bring literally multitudes to Christ. But something has happened in the church: We've sold out to the world. Even the *Wall Street Journal* noted this with its article on April 23, 1999, titled, "Singing Songs of Love, Not God." This article subtitled "This Is Christian Music?" speaks at length of the commercialization of contemporary Christian music, and the stark lack of clarity in the message from many of today's top Christian musicians.

Today secular companies have bought most of the Christian music labels. Many Christian bands have watered down their message for fear it will not be a good sell. In business school, they call this marketing.

Paul wrote these clarifying words to the first-century church at Corinth: "That ye may be blameless and harmless, the sons of God, without rebuke, in the midst of a crooked and perverse nation, among whom ye shine as lights in the world." (2 Corinthians 2:17)

This verse speaks about making merchandise of the Gospel. Although this verse does not specifically mention music, the principle is clear: Ministry is not a business venture.

God never raised music to be marketable. God raised music to be a ministry to the hearts and lives of people and to see them transformed by His grace.

In Conclusion

In this brief study, we have looked at the purpose, pitfalls, and principles for music. The goal of this study has been to be fair yet thoroughly biblical in our approach to music. As you consider these words, I trust that you will do so with your heart and life open to God and allow His Spirit to guide your understanding for His glory.

Having come to the end, here is where the rubber meets the road. Consider the following questions prayerfully:

- Has your purpose for music measured up? Do you see music as a means of glorifying God, or is it simply entertainment?
- How about the pitfalls? Have you become snared, or are you aware of and avoiding these common traps?
- What are your principles for music? Take time to write them out for your own good. Would you then measure them against the Word of God?

Lastly, when making your choices on music, consider

1. Lyrics

This is the message you want to communicate. In a study of the history of Christian music, it can be readily seen that lyrics had scriptural and theological weight and became another way to transfer God's truth to man's heart. They were not given to the seven eleven choruses we see so often today. Eleven? Yes, seven words sung eleven times.

2. Music

The music is a platform or a vehicle by which means the message of the lyrics is delivered. The music should not be in a counter position to the lyrics.

3. Instruments

Today many times the instruments are so loud that they totally block the communication of the message of the lyrics and become a detriment, appealing only to the flesh and not the Spirit.

Now honestly ask yourself the following questions:

*   Does it glorify God? – 1 Corinthians 10:31
*   Is it grounded in truth? – Ephesians 5:19
*   Does it produce godliness? – 1 Corinthians 10:23
*   Is it without guile? – 1 Corinthians 8:9
*   Is it for personal gain? – 2 Corinthians 2:17

I am deeply burdened as I see biblical principles ignored under the guise of a changing culture, changes forgetting that the purpose of church music is to honor God and glorify His name.

Also, in many cases, instead of fathers training their children godly principles, children change their fathers, disregarding their lifetime of Christian ministry.

Chapter Eleven

What Would Jesus Do: Will You Follow His Steps?

What comes to your mind when you think about the life of Christ?

A few years ago at a NBA playoff game, a great truth came into view. A certain player came down the court with the ball, pulled up, and shot a perfect jump shot. The crowd went wild with enthusiasm. As this player turned to run down the court, the camera focused in on his wrist and revealed a wristband with the inscription "WWJD?" which stands for "What would Jesus do?" Now you could say, "Hallelujah, praise the Lord!" But the camera continued to pan across this individual, and into view came suggestive tattoos, earrings, and various images all over his body. I would add that even though we see many Christians wearing tattoos today, I am reminded that tattoos came from aspects of pagan and demon worship. What a confusing scenario!

Famous witch and author Laurie Cabot writes of the tattoo: "The origins of tattooing came from ancient magical practices . . ."[1]

Again, remember with me what Jack Wyrtzen once said, "I believe the generation we're living in can be underscored by two words: compromise and confusion."

This is just one example, but there are countless other athletes and high-profile people who use this little wristband almost as a good-luck charm. We need to ask ourselves, what does WWJD mean? What is this all about, and does the Bible have anything to say about what Jesus would do? A very important passage of Scripture on this matter is found in the first letter of Peter:

"Servants, be subject to your masters with all fear; not only to the good and gentle, but also to the froward. For this is thankworthy, if a man for conscience toward God endure grief, suffering wrongfully. For what glory is it, if, when ye be buffeted for your faults, ye shall take it patiently? but if, when ye do well, and suffer for it, ye take it patiently, this is acceptable with God. For even hereunto were ye called: because Christ also suffered for us, leaving us an example, that ye should follow his steps: Who did no sin, neither was guile found in his mouth: Who, when he was reviled, reviled not again; when he suffered, he threatened not; but committed himself to him that judgeth righteously: Who his own self bare our sins in his own body on the tree, that we, being dead to sins, should live unto righteousness: by whose stripes ye were healed. For ye were as sheep going astray; but are now returned unto the Shepherd and Bishop of your souls." (1 Peter 2:18-25)

WWJD—what would Jesus do? The apostle Peter is speaking about a very important issue. It's interesting to note that many people today wear the wristband WWJD but have no concept of what it really means to live and act as Jesus did.

As we look on this passage in 1 Peter, we see a very interesting phrase right in the middle: "Christ also suffered for us leaving us an example."

This is a very interesting term, *leaving for us an example*. This term was used for one who would give an outline to be traced. A young child who was learning the process of writing would be given a very clear pattern. Over the top of that pattern, the child placed transparent paper and traced the outline of the image below. This term was also used in architecture. An architect would have a pattern and very carefully trace the lines under that pattern. What the apostle Peter is saying is that Christ left something very clear to be traced. He left His example as a pattern.

Maybe, as a child, you wandered into your dad's closet and slipped into his shoes and began to walk. His shoes were big and rather clunky, but you took some steps. You were in his shoes, taking his steps. That's the concept here—walking in His steps, tracing the pattern, taking every precaution not to go outside the lines, but to follow His impression carefully.

WWJD? What would Jesus do? As you look into the context of this passage, you can see very clearly certain things that Jesus would do. These are things, to be sure, most NBA athletes would never think about doing. What are they?

Unjust Suffering

Number one, Jesus would take unjust suffering. In this portion of Scripture, Peter is writing to those who are actually slaves. These slaves had put their faith in Christ and now were struggling because, even though they had been freed by Christ, they were still slaves. They wondered, "What would Jesus do? What should our attitude be toward our masters?" Peter shows what our attitudes should be if we receive unjust suffering as we serve Christ. Look again at the text: "Servants, be subject to your masters with all fear; not only to the good and gentle, but also to the froward." (1 Peter 2:18)

Do you know what he is saying? As you are living out the whole concept of WWJD, walking in His steps, tracing the pattern, many times you may have to take unjust suffering. Peter goes on to say, "What glory is it, if, when ye be buffeted for your faults, ye shall take it patiently?" (1 Peter 2:20)

If you are doing wrong and suffer, there is no praise. But if you are doing right, carrying out everything properly, and patiently enduring suffering, there is much praise before God. Think about it—that's what Jesus did.

Isaiah the prophet speaks clearly about the vicarious sufferings of Christ in Isaiah 53. There, we read, "And he opened not his mouth."

Some time ago, I stood with a small group of our staff at the ancient city of Philippi. We were shooting video for a project on the journeys of the apostle Paul. The backdrop was to tell where the apostle Paul had been imprisoned. He was imprisoned unjustly, but what was Paul's attitude? Was he grumbling and moaning? No, there he was at midnight, in stocks, along with Silas; and they were singing praises to God.

WWJD? What does it mean? It means knowing how to suffer unjustly. When you have done everything right and you still take the hit for it, when you trace out the pattern perfectly and you are still accused falsely, when you walk ever so carefully and people still slap you in the face, you do not retaliate.

Most have watched the NBA playoffs. Does the referee ever get the call right? No matter what he calls, it's wrong to one team or the other. The coach jumps, rants, and raves. The players often get right in the referee's face. But you will observe that a real champion knows how to take it when he gets a wrong call.

Have you been the recipient of some wrong calls? WWJD? What does it really mean to take it patiently?

Every year each member of our staff has a job review. Maybe you can relate, remembering a time when your work was reviewed and you thought to yourself, "I deserve a better review than that. They're judging me unjustly!" WWJD? What would Jesus do? He took it patiently. He took it in stride.

Champion athletes know how to take wrong calls in stride and keep on going for victory.

Unquestionable Submission

WWJD? As we consider this question, we will see it is not only a matter of unjust suffering, but it is also a demonstration of unquestionable submission. Look back at the text found in 1 Peter 2:23: "Who, when he was reviled, reviled not again; when he suffered, he threatened not; but committed himself to him that judgeth righteously."

Of all people who could threaten, the Lord could back it up. Go ahead and slap me, but rest assured, one day, the other shoe will drop. Remember, it is Peter who is writing. He really learned a lesson from the Lord. When Peter was with Christ in the garden and the soldiers came to arrest Jesus, the first thing Peter did was to draw his sword and cut off Malcus's ear. The Lord told Peter to put away his sword. Jesus could take care of Himself. He did not need Peter's sword. He, if need be, could call legions of angels. Jesus did not come to destroy people—He came to bring them to Himself. The verse concludes with this awesome phrase: "But committed himself to him that judges righteously."

WWJD? What is it all about? Unquestionable submission. You commit yourself to a sovereign God—The One who never makes a bad call, The One who knows the end from the beginning.

Paul, writing about having a proper attitude, says, "Let this mind be in you, which was also in Christ Jesus: Who, being in the form of God, thought it not robbery to be equal with God: But made himself of no reputation, and took upon him the form of a servant, and was made in the likeness of men." (Philippians 2:5-7)

"But made himself of no reputation" translates from the Greek word *knosis*. The root idea is "He emptied Himself." What's that all about? Did He lay aside His deity? Never! What we see here is unquestionable submission to a sovereign God, giving up His rights and divine prerogatives. That's WWJD.

Have you taken that step—the step of unquestionable submission? Have you committed your life to Him, the One who knows every circumstance and never makes a bad call? When those around you make seemingly bad calls, do you have unquestionable submission to Christ? What a blessing it is to observe this whole concept fleshed out in people's lives. Are you fleshing it out, walking in His steps? WWJD?

Unjust suffering, unquestionable submission, and then there is the matter of unlimited service.

Unlimited Service

Remember, Peter is writing to slaves. A slave did not have the liberty to say, "No, I'm not going to work this hour or lift that particular stone. I'm not going to do it."

Some of the amazing things you will see as you go to Israel or visit some of the ancient sites of Greece or Rome are the huge edifices built from mammoth stones. These stones are stacked one upon other. As you marvel at the construction, you will stop and ask yourself, how in the world did they ever get those huge stones there? The answer: slave labor. It is amazing to note there were sixty million slaves in the Roman Empire.

In this passage, Peter is using the concept of a slave to illustrate how we must approach our service to God. He is saying that you must have unlimited service. Slaves cannot serve their masters just when they think they're doing what is good for them. A slave must serve even the froward, even those who are cruel and wicked. If you approach serving Christ as a slave would, you will serve with unlimited service because your service is dedicated to God.

We need to have our focus go beyond the immediate to the eternal. We must stop and consider that our service is not just for this human leader, this teacher, or this parent but for God. It's unlimited service.

Again, Paul, as he wrote to the church at Philippi, said that Christ *took upon himself the form of a servant* (Philippians 2:7). The form of a servant—Paul took that concept from the words of Jesus Christ Himself. In Mark 10, Jesus is handling a squabble between His disciples over who is greatest. Note Christ's words: "And whosoever of you will be the chiefest, shall be servant of all. For even the Son of man came not to be ministered unto, but to minister, and to give his life a ransom for many." (Mark 10:44-45)

Throughout His life, Jesus lived the example of servanthood. You will recall the scene that occurred the night before the cross. There, in the upper room, the disciples are still squabbling about the chief places, the places of greatest importance. Quietly, Jesus assumes the role of a servant. He takes a basin and starts to wash the disciples' feet. What an awesome illustration!

Does your service stop short of this example? Are you the type of person who says, "I'm not going to wash that person's feet! I'm not going to humble myself to do that task. Don't you know my position?" WWJD? What was His position? He is the Lord of Glory! Yet He would take upon Himself a task that His disciples wouldn't think of doing.

Among those who work with top athletes, there's a common word used to describe these superstars: prima donna. A prima donna wants everything done for him.

In an interview after his last NBA game, Jeff Hornacek said that the most important thing to him was his family. Game after game, you would see him with his wife and little girls. When he came to a game, it was not in a stretch limo but rather in a Dodge Caravan with his wife and kids. In another interview, he made this statement: "My life in basketball has not been about stardom but about serving the team." Is that your concept? Unlimited service? WWJD?

Unconditional Sacrifice

As we read about the very person of Jesus Christ and that awesome passage in Philippians 2:5-8, we read these words, "And was made in the likeness of men: And being found in fashion as a man, he humbled himself, and became obedient unto death, even the death of the cross."

Unconditional sacrifice. *Even the death of the cross.* Consider the example of Jesus Christ. WWJD? What would Jesus do? He'd be a sacrifice. He would give His life as a ransom for many. But now consider how He did it. In the Gospel of John 10, Jesus said that no man took His life from Him but that He laid it down of His own accord. It was a voluntary sacrifice. He wasn't forced. He did it of His own free will. WWJD means that by an act of my own will, I give myself as a sacrifice for others.

I think today we have wrong ideas about leadership. Jesus Christ said that the greatest leader is the greatest servant. That means longer hours. That means constantly giving of yourself. That means really placing your head on a chopping block. Unconditional sacrifice is awesome. If you want to wear that little wristband, WWJD, then think about what comes along with that—unconditional sacrifice.

We've considered walking in His steps, tracing His outline, and we see, first, unjust suffering; second, unquestionable submission; third, unlimited service; and fourth, unconditional sacrifice. Having read this far, one might say, "That's pretty dull. What comes out of a lifestyle like that?"

Unending Satisfaction

Here is the answer: unending satisfaction. Don't ever let the devil box you out and make you think that walking in the steps of Jesus Christ doesn't have at its end something so awesome, so wonderful, so amazing, that the devil and all his hosts could never give you even a small percentage of it. Listen to these words from the writer to the Hebrews:

> "Looking unto Jesus the author and finisher of our faith; who for the joy that was set before him endured the cross, despising the shame, and is set down at the right hand of the throne of God." (Hebrews 12:2)

The writer to the Hebrews said that he looked down that road and saw at the end *unending satisfaction.*

Jesus Christ said, "And he that sent me is with me: the Father hath not left me alone; for I do always those things that please him." (John 8:39)

What an awesome statement!

In chapter four, Jesus's disciples had gone out to find food, and He was there with the Samaritan woman, sharing something better than any sparkling water on the market today—it was living water. The disciples came back and were astonished that He was talking with a woman. They said, "Master, eat." But Jesus replied, "I have meat to eat ye know not of." His meat was doing the will of God.

Have you ever thought about the will of God in those terms? It strengthens, it sustains, and it satisfies. Doing the will of God has a greater lasting satisfaction than anything the world, the flesh, or the devil could ever offer you. Unending satisfaction.

I had the privilege of observing Jack Wyrtzen for years. As I observed him, I always saw a man who was full of joy. As a young man, that was so attractive to me. I saw this man full of life, full of joy, and I said, "I want that, that unending satisfaction!" Where did it come from? It came from doing the will of God.

WWJD? What would Jesus do? Jesus would get His satisfaction from doing the will of God and not living for the lust of the flesh, the lust of the eyes, and the pride of life.

At a previous conference for those who direct the various works of Word of Life around the world, Harry Bollback, who, along with Jack Wyrtzen, founded the ministry of Word of Life, was sharing and said, "WWJD?" Then he went on to clarify that what he meant was not "What would Jesus do?" but rather "What would Joe do?" Now that hit me wrong at first, but then I began to think about it. Would I shrink from giving an example that people could follow? Isn't that the issue? What would I do? What about you?

As you have read these words, the question for you is, what would you do? Put your initials there—WW _ D? Walking in His steps, what would you do? You might think, "That's too much for me, I can't do it." But there is good news. In 1 Peter 2:19, 20, it begins with "For this is thankworthy." This word, "thankworthy," is the same word translated as "grace" in other places. Now look back to the last part of verse 20: "But if, when ye do well, and suffer for it, ye take patiently, this is acceptable with God."

Do you know how you can do this? By the grace of God. That's what the writer is saying. You say, "I could never measure up to that!" You're right, but through God's grace, you can. Peter writes that if someone is treated wrongfully and they take it patiently, this is an evidence of the grace of God.

Dear one, WWJD is not just a bracelet that you wear around your wrist. Rather, it is a band you wear around your heart. You may be thinking, "God, I don't want to go outside the lines. I want to trace it out just right, but I can't do it in and of myself. I can, however, do it through your grace, and I know that the full measure of grace that came to me at salvation is sufficient now for my service."

Remember, WWJD?

Chapter Twelve

The Choice of a Lifetime: Biblical Principles for Choosing a Life Mate

Political elections are often very close. The choice of just the right man is important, and as a nation, we live with our choice. We live with some choices for four years and others for six. Sometimes, after only a few weeks or months, we regret the choice we have made, but we have to live with the official we have elected.

Apart from trusting Christ, the most important choice each person makes is the choice of a life partner. That choice is not a choice for four or even six years but, rather, a choice that will last a lifetime.

When approaching any important decision, the first question we should ask is, what does the Bible say? Let's consider these words found in Proverbs 18:22: "Whoso findeth a wife findeth a good thing, and obtaineth favour of the Lord."

In his classic commentary on the book of Proverbs, Charles Bridges says, "This is obviously to be taken within certain limits. Manoah found a good thing in his wife (Judges 13:23), but Job did not (Job 2:9-10). To some their wives are a crown for their heads, while others find that their wives rot their bones (12:4)."

What is *good* implies godliness. Godliness is found when the man marries in the Lord and only one who is the Lord's. To be unequally yoked with an unbeliever (2 Corinthians 6:14), union for life between a child of God and a child of Satan is a most dreadful anomaly. "I wish," said pious Bishop Hall, "that Manoah could speak so loud that all our Israelites could hear him: 'Is there never a woman among the daughters of thy brethren, or among all God's people, that thou goest to take a wife of the uncircumcised Philistines?' If religion be anything other than a cipher, how dare we not regard it in our most important choice? Is she a fair Philistine? Why is not the deformity of the soul more powerful to dissuade us than the beauty of the face to allure us?"[1]

Several years ago, I spoke on this verse to a group of several hundred. After the service, I heard a couple of young men talking, and one asked the other, "Have you found any good thing yet?"

A girl who overheard him got upset and said, "Listen, I want to tell you I'm more than a thing!"

To which he replied, "You'd better believe that!"

As God is speaking in this verse through the wise man, He is speaking about a vital choice in life, the choice of a wife. As you consider the words of this passage, consider also some words from the great expositor Martin Lloyd Jones. Writing about the choice of a wife, he says, "Make sure you have a Christian view of marriage because it is unique. It is a view entirely different from any other, because it is a view found only in the Bible." He goes on to say, "Unsavory though it might seem, I must say the common view of marriage is purely a physical one. It is something that is based almost exclusively on physical attraction and the desire for physical gratification. It is a legalization of physical attraction and physical gratification.

So often the sacred union of marriage is treated like nothing but that; hence the scandal of mounting divorce. The parties have not even thought about it. They have no view of marriage at all. They are governed entirely by animal instincts and impulses. The marriage is a union based purely on the physical and never rises above it. There is no thought whatsoever of marriage in and of itself. It is only the thought of legalizing something they want to do. Your choice must go beyond "skin deep"![2]

In Proverbs 18:22, the writer says that a wife is good, not gratifying. She is more than gratifying—she is good.

Charles Bridges continues saying, "Some find a crown to their head as they find a wife; others find rottenness to their bones. That which alone deserves the name wife is a good thing. If, in the state of innocence, it was not good for man to be alone, much more in a world of care and trouble two are better than one for mutual support and helpfulness and sympathy. The good thing implies godliness and fitness. When we choose, why is it not the deformity of the soul which powerfully dissuades us instead of the beauty of the face which powerfully allures us?"[3] Tremendous words, but how does one go about making such a choice?

Because of the drives God built into every young man and young woman, taking notice of the opposite sex is a normal response. But how do you see them? What are you looking for? What is the first thing you focus on? And why? For what? What is their allurement? Is it strictly physical as we read in the quote from Martin Lloyd Jones? Is it just looking for something to satisfy physical desire, or is your desire to have the mate God would have for you?

As we consider the truth, "He that findeth a wife findeth a good thing," we see in Scripture that some made good choices and others made bad choices. I think of Manoah—he found a good thing. You can read about his choice in Judges 13. Job, on the other hand, as we see in Job 2:9, made a choice that was not so good. Job's wife encouraged him to curse God and die. How would you like to live with a spouse like that throughout your whole life—the kind of spouse who spends his or her days and energies, suggestions, and powers of persuasion trying to get you to turn against the revealed will of God? That's a bad choice.

Samson made another bad choice when he said to his parents, "I have seen a woman in Timnath of the daughters of the Philistines: now therefore get her for me to wife." (Judges 14:2)

What is Samson saying. Look closely at his words: "She excites me! She gratifies my senses. Get her for me!"

Samson's parents reply, "Is there never a woman among the daughters of thy brethren, or among all my people, that thou goest to take a wife of the uncircumcised Philistines?"

But Samson demands, "Get her for me; for she pleaseth me well."

Through the years, I've watched how couples come together. It's interesting, but the little phrase "birds of a feather flock together" usually holds true. However, sometimes a wonderful girl is lured away by some strange bird, and the result is a foul deal.

The apostle Paul gives us some insight in the letter he writes to the church at Corinth. In 2 Corinthians 6:14, Paul writes, "Be not ye unequally yoked together with unbelievers."

It is interesting to think about the different messages you remember. I guarantee you there will be some messages you will hear and remember the rest of your life; others you won't even remember the next day.

When I was working on Word of Life Island many years ago, Dr. Charles Ryrie was there and spoke to a small group of young people enjoying ice cream on a little float boat. As Dr. Ryrie spoke to this small group of around twenty young adults, he asked this question concerning the choice of a wife: "Does the choice fit?" I remember those words very clearly because, at that time, I was dating a wonderful Christian girl who loved the Lord. However, the more I thought about what he was saying and the more I examined our relationship in light of his message, the more I was persuaded of God that the choice did not fit.

As you read this, I want you to determine that you will let the Bible serve as your guide for one of the most important choices of your life: the choice of a wife or the choice of a husband. As you make this decision, carefully consider what the Bible says about not being unequally yoked.

Same Destiny

Look to your destiny. When a person trusts Christ as his Savior, that decision changes forever their destiny. There have been young people who have given their hearts to someone who had a different destiny with tragic results. The importance of having the same destiny may seem basic, but it should bind every thought you have.

Same Direction

The second question one should ask is, are we going in the same direction? When I was in college and became convinced of the importance of going the same direction, I quietly watched certain young ladies who were of some attraction to me. I watched, but I watched from a distance. People are smarter than you think. Roommates talk. Sometimes they want to help your situation, but in the end, they hurt.

At college, I watched carefully to see which girls went to a student activity called SMF (Student Missionary Fellowship). SMF met on Wednesday nights, and attendance was optional. I watched to see which girls went. If I saw a girl who I might be interested in and she had no interest in SMF, I mentally crossed her off. She no longer interested me. I watched from a distance. Why? I knew God was leading me to the mission field, and I wanted to find a girl going in the same direction. After I settled that, I started observing other areas of her life.

Same Devotion

The third area of consideration is devotion. I watched how the young lady handled her Bible. This might sound strange, but I look at my Bible as a love letter from Jesus.

I'm married now to a godly lady, but when I was in high school and college, I was so focused on this that I wouldn't even talk to a young lady if she hadn't had her devotions or her quiet time. If she approached me and said something, I'd ask her, "How did your quiet time go?" If she replied, "Well, I haven't had it yet," my response was, "Well, I'm sorry, but it is better for you to talk to God before you talk to me." This was serious.

I watched, trying not to be obvious. I would ask a girl if I could look at her Bible. I watched the way she responded to my interest in her spiritual life and listened to her answers to my questions. I began doing this in high school. I watched to see if she brought her Bible to school, but I also watched where she put her Bible. I was never interested in anyone who put another book on top of her Bible. This was God's Holy Word. I was never interested in a girl who threw her Bible on the ground. I listened to the way she talked about Jesus.

The song says, "My Jesus I love thee I know thou art mine. For thee all the follies of sin I resign."

Devotion was very, very important to me. If she didn't love Jesus passionately, she could never love me permanently. The same devotion, that godly devotion, is the bottom line.

Ladies, you can do that with the guys too—it's a two-way street, perhaps maybe even more so with you because the man is to be the spiritual leader.

Same Desires

What about this equal yoke? Destiny, direction, devotion, also desires. What type of desires?

I was interested in one young lady who went to SMF, and so we sat together. In the middle of the meeting, I looked in her direction and saw she was asleep. That was the last time I asked her out. I thought that if she did not have any more interest in God's Word than that, she did not share my desire. This may seem drastic to you, but I'm just sharing my heart.

I don't know what desires you have, but the desires you share with your spouse must mesh. Do you know what starts happening with desires? You begin to talk about them, and if they don't fit, you are in trouble.

Same Duty

Finally, in this area of being equally yoked, you also must have the same duty or diligence.

As you look through the book of Proverbs, a subject we are often warned about is laziness. Do you ever watch a person's work or study habits? This thing of duty and diligence is very important and must mesh.

As you think about duty, I want to draw your attention to one who did find a good thing. His account is located in Genesis 24. His name is Isaac, and we can learn a lot from him. How did he do it? If we were to ask him, "Isaac, how did you do it?" he would more than likely reply, "I did it through prayer." Isaac found his wife as he was committed diligently in prayer to his God. As he prayed, his heart became in tune with God's will for him.

Are you praying this kind of fervent prayer, "God, tune up my heart, transform my value system, help me to focus on the right things"?

With Isaac, I also notice that he not only depended on God but also trusted his spiritual leadership. Did you know that it was his father's servant who selected his wife? That is a foreign concept in our society and not one I am suggesting we adopt, but are you ready to let one of your dad's godly friends pick out your wife? I doubt if any would be so trusting.

Dependence on spiritual leadership—Abraham's servant looked to God to guide him to the right wife for Isaac. This is a good principle. Find a spiritual leader whom you are close enough with to ask his opinion.

Do not opt for this worldly "I don't care what anyone says. There she is, get her for me" attitude, which was Samson's approach. Samson really got messed up because he didn't listen to spiritual leadership. On the other hand, Isaac listened, and he waited upon God. Don't be in a hurry!

Some young adults behave as if they think the assembly line is going to stop and there won't be anyone left. They think, "If I don't get a wife or a husband now, I'll be left out."

Jack Wyrtzen said many times, "Single blessedness is better than double cussedness." This was Jacks' special way of saying it is better to be single in the will of God than to be married out of the will of God. Wait on God.

Perhaps this seems too heavenly-minded, but God knows your need of a spouse. God is not a sadist or an ascetic. His timetable is best. Wait on God.

Finally, we can observe from the choice made by Isaac that we can't get physically involved, allowing our emotions and our passions to control our hearts. Back off! Allow God to inflame your heart with holy desires, not fleshly physical passion.

Maybe our desire should be that which is expressed in Psalm 47:4: "He shall choose our inheritance for us."

I like that. God will choose my inheritance for me.

Let's look beyond the face and beyond the figure to the facts—facts like conversion, commitment, compassion, and finally, complement.

The word "help meet" means "complement." She is a complement to you. Will she complement you or complicate you? He that findeth a wife, God says, findeth a treasure.

Now some of the girls might say, "That's great, but some of us feel like hidden treasures. Who's going to discover us?"

> "The eye of the Lord runneth to and fro." (2 Chronicles 16:9)

If you're discovered for the wrong reasons, the relationship will not be a blessing in your life but, rather, a blight. You need to wait and be discovered for the right reasons, and God will use you as an awesome complement.

Life is filled with choices. On election day, our nation makes choices. We live with some for four years and some for six years, but one day you will make a choice that you'll live with for the rest of your life.

My prayer is that you'll make it according to the Word of God and in such a way that, as the years roll by, you'll say, "Praise God for the wonderful wife or husband He sent my way!"

My heart can echo that, and I give testimony to a wonderful, godly wife—a wonderful woman who is my treasure and my complement.

I'm a satisfied customer, and that's what I desire for each of you who read these words—that you will make choices according to God's Word, which will lead to a life of satisfaction and joy in your marriage.

Chapter Thirteen

Profiting from Prophecy: How to Correctly View Prophetic Truth

"If you can look into the seeds of time, and say which grain will grow and which will not; speak then to me."[1]

These words penned by William Shakespeare in *Macbeth* pose a question concerning prophecy and its value to man. Shakespeare, of course, had no concept of the profitability of the only type of prophecy that truly matters and is truly reliable—Bible prophecy. Yet the question is posed in what will Bible prophecies bring profit to the lives of those who are engaged in its study?

As the aged apostle Paul was nearing the end of his life, the Spirit of God guided him to direct his last letter to young Timothy. In 2 Timothy 3, after speaking of the last days (the period between the time of the writing of the apostle's letter and the Lord's return) with all its dangers, he points to the profitability of the Scripture when he said, "All Scripture is given by inspiration of God, and is profitable." (2 Timothy 3:16)

The word "profitable" in this text speaks of something useful, helpful, or advantageous. Without a doubt, we can say that prophecy, truly, is profitable because approximately one-fourth of all Scripture was prophetic when it was written. It is useful, it is helpful, and it is advantageous. To eliminate the study of prophecy would be to eliminate a great portion of our Bible.

Sadly, because of an Athenian spirit (the desire just to hear something new solely for the purpose of satiating one's carnal curiosity or intellect), the present generation has deemed the study of prophecy irrelevant for the present-day church. Yet a study of church history and the Scriptures would show otherwise. If there ever was a day when the church of the Lord Jesus Christ needed to know God's purposes and plan for our future, it is today. Although there are many ways a proper study of prophecy can bring much profit to the church, we will highlight three key areas that are vital to the life of the believer in Christ.

The first area examines the problem of ignorance of the Scriptures, the Word of God. The second area considers our service for God (the work of God) and addresses the problem of inactivity. The third area focuses on our Savior (the worship of God) and critiques the problem of indifference.

The Scriptures: The Problem of Ignorance

It is impossible for one to have a complete view of the Scriptures and the knowledge of God without having a complete view of prophecy. One of God's key purposes of prophecy is to reveal to us what will happen before it happens. By the sheer fact of the abundance of space that the Spirit of God devotes to prophecy, it is easy to see the importance God gives to this vital truth.

Thinking about prophecy and focusing on the Second Coming of Christ in Scripture, we observe the following statistics:

- Approximately one-fourth of the Bible was prophetic when it was written.
- Of the 333 prophecies concerning Christ, only 109 of them were fulfilled at His First Coming, leaving 224 yet to be fulfilled at His Second Coming.
- Three are a total of 1,527 Old Testament passages referring to the Second Coming.
- In the New Testament, 330 verses refer directly to the Second Coming of Christ.
- The Lord Himself refers to His return twenty-one times in Scripture.

To be ignorant of such a significant amount of the Word of God opens the door to all types of false doctrines and false hopes. As the apostle Paul wrote to the church of Thessalonica, "I would not have you to be ignorant, brethren . . ." (1 Thessalonians 4:13)

Because the believers of Thessalonica were very concerned about their loved ones who had died, several questions came to their minds: What would happen to them should the Lord return? What would happen to their dead loved ones in Christ?

This prophetic portion of Paul's letter to the Thessalonian church was designed to remove their ignorance concerning the return of Christ, the resurrection of the dead in Christ, and the rapture of the church.

The profit that this knowledge brought to the Thessalonian believers can be ours too as we commit our heart and minds to the study of the prophetic Word. The words of C. I. Scofield support this truth:

> "We open pages of the prophetic Word, and we see passing before us the magnificent panorama of the future of the nations. Our God unfolds to us that which He is doing here and there in this world; and not only that, He lifts the veil and shows us that which He is going to do in the future. Through the prophetic Word, and through that alone, we look over into the great hereafter, and see that which is to be. We look into an open Heaven with all its joys and glories, the goal of our own desire; and we look into an open hell. All this is in the prophetic Word. The mightiest subjects, the greatest thoughts that can possibly fill the mind are those with which the prophetic Word is occupied."[2]

The proper study of prophecy also sheds light on false prophets and their heretical teachings. Concerning these false prophets, the apostle Peter said, "Knowing this first, that there shall come in the last days scoffers, walking after their own lusts, and saying, Where is the promise of his coming? for since the fathers fell asleep, all things continue as they were from the beginning of creation." (2 Peter 3:3, 4)

Speaking about this portion of Scripture, E. Schuyler English said,

> "The last days are already here, dear friends, but we are not in the darkness that the day of the Lord's coming should overtake us as a thief. Through reading the Scriptures, we have been permitted to step behind the

curtain of the future to discover ahead of time how the drama begins and unfolds."[3]

Without a doubt, one of the great advantages of studying prophecy is that it helps remove our ignorance concerning the Scriptures, protecting us from destructive heresies. In a day of such insecurity, the study of prophecy underlines the authority of God's Word and gives us the assurance and comfort we need.

The importance of addressing the problem of ignorance is demonstrated by the ministry of the apostle in Thessalonica, where he possibly remained only three or four weeks. Yet, in that period, Paul gave them an extensive study in prophecy.

Lewis Sperry Chafer refers to this in his introduction to eschatology:

> "In the limited time of his stay in that city, he was confronted with heathenism but was able to make contacts with individuals and not only to lead them to Christ but to teach them enough truth that he would afterwards write the two Thessalonian Epistles to them with the expectation that they would understand them. In the second Epistle where the reference is made to the falling away, the 'man of sin' who will sit in the restored Jewish temple declaring himself to be God and the destruction of the 'man of sin' by the glorious appearing of Christ, Paul declares 'remember ye not that when I was yet with you I told you these things.' Assuredly, no clear evidence could be desired to establish the truth that both Christ and Paul gave to the right understanding of prophecy a foremost place. There is no license granted here for a teacher to be a faddist in prophetic truth, nor is there any permission granted to men to ignore the field of prophetic revelation."[4]

A thorough study of prophecy addresses the problem of ignorance of God's Word and also forms a barricade against the barrage of false teaching from the many cults that have invaded Christendom today.

Dave Breese says in his book, *The Marks of a Cult*,

> "The chief reason for the success of cults is the spiritual naiveté on the part of people. Far too many Christians are content with the superficial knowledge of the Word of God, thinking themselves spiritually intelligent. Nothing could be further from the truth. The Christian must give himself to a detailed study of Scripture and understand the Bible from a doctrinal point of view."[5]

Thinking of the tremendous profit of prophecy in relation to the Scriptures, the words of the apostle Paul to young Timothy are very apropos: "Study to shew thyself approved unto God, a workman that needeth not to be ashamed, rightly dividing the word of truth." (2 Timothy 2:15)

To truly profit from prophecy, it is important to note different schools of theology in this area:

1. Postmillennialism

The main idea of this view is that the Gospel will triumph and bring in the second coming of Christ. So that means the return of Christ will come after the millennium.

The main proponents of this view were Charles Hodge and A. H. Strong. This position is rarely seen in theological circles today.

2. Amillennialism

Simply stated, the letter "A" means "no"; that is to say no millennium. This means they propound that there will be no literal earthly reign of Christ for the thousand years as stated in Revelation 20 six times. They just spiritualize the text, saying the reign of Christ is in the heart of the believer, not on planet Earth. This school of thought historically started with Augustine in the fourth and fifth century AD.

Noted scholars who hold to this position were Louis Berkhof, William Hendrickson, and Lenkski.

Both of these positions do not handle the texts concerning the reign of Christ in a literal way. Their hermeneutics do not contemplate a literal fulfillment of God's promise to King David as we see in 2 Samuel 7:12-16.

If one takes that position of seeing that promise as the reign of Christ in man's heart, he can have no assurance of our Lord's promise of a literal heaven as a real place for real people.

3. Premillennialism

This school of biblical interpretation states that there will be a literal return of Christ to earth to establish His long promised earthly reign, fulfilling the "Davidic Covenant." It is called premillennialism because it emphasizes "pre" or before the millennium, holding to the return of Messiah before the establishment of His earthly reign. There are a number of renown theologians, whom I have had the privilege of calling my friends, who hold this position, namely Charles C. Ryrie, Dwight Pentecost, John Walvoord, Stanley Toussaint, Lehman Strauss, and Paige Patterson.

Other notable men of God included in this list are C. I. Scofield, H. A. Ironside, William Pettingill, Alva McClain, Griffith Thomas, Charles Feinberg, and Louis Sperry Chafer.

For those who call this position a recent one, it is noteworthy that early church fathers, such as Papias of Hierapolis and Justin Martyr, taught these great truths.

But the most important proof is Scripture itself. We see this truth clearly presented in many books in the Bible as the Psalms, Isaiah, Jeremiah, Daniel, Hosea, Amos, and through the Old Testament prophets. In the New Testament, it is taught in Matthew, Acts, Romans, Jude, and the book of Revelation.

The Service of God: The Problem of Inactivity

The next benefit from a proper study of Bible prophecy is that it addresses the problem of inactivity in the work of God. As we study the great prophecies of the coming of our Lord Jesus Christ, we are moved to action. The study of prophecy should not produce a divisive spirit or a dormant spirit but a dynamic spirit resulting in service for our Lord. Some of the greatest evangelistic and missionary movements in this past century were born out of great prophetic conferences that motivated the participants of those conferences to share their faith and sound out the message of the coming of Christ. The truth that the study of prophecy should produce not inactivity but activity is underscored through Paul's very stern admonition in 2 Thessalonians 3:6, where he says, "Now we command you, brethren, in the name of our Lord Jesus Christ, that ye withdraw yourselves from every brother that walketh disorderly, and not after the tradition which he received of us."

Some members of the church at Thessalonica took the study of prophecy and the return of Christ as an opportunity for inactivity, leaving their jobs and living off the church. This was met with a strong word of correction from the apostle Paul, saying that those who did not work must not eat. Prophecy should never produce laziness or inactivity. Concerning this truth, Warren Wiersbe says,

> "Misinterpretations and misapplications of the truths of God's Word can cause endless trouble. History records the foolishness of people who set dates, sell their possessions and sit on mountains waiting for the Lord to return. Any teaching that encourages us to disobey another divine teaching is not Bible teaching."[6]

Paul goes on to say in 2 Thessalonians 3:11, "For we hear that there are some which walk among you disorderly, working not at all, but are busybodies."

Not only does the proper study of prophecy produce work or service for God, but it also produces the right type of work. Interestingly, we see in this text a play on words because the word "busybody" means to work all around, bustle about, to be occupied but as busy bodies—that is, everywhere doing everything but accomplishing nothing. An important benefit of prophetic study is that it produces not busybodies but people who are busy in the body of Christ, building it up, not burdening it down. This great truth is underscored as Paul writes to the church at Rome, saying, "And that, knowing the time, that now it is high time to awake out of sleep: for now is our salvation nearer than when we believed." (Romans 13:11)

The understanding of the future culmination of our salvation at the return of our Lord Jesus Christ should motivate us to a life of productivity and purity. This was the very heartbeat of Paul as he wrote to Titus in Titus 2:11-15.

The study of prophecy is totally related to our spiritual walk and our work for Christ in this present age. Academics should never be divorced from activity in the service of our Savior. Dr. Roy B. Zuck says it well: "To have the academic without the spiritual is like having a car without gasoline or like having wood on a cold day with no match for a fire."[7]

B. B. Warfield said it another way: "Knowledge of the Word is a powerful thing . . . and so is a locomotive a powerful thing providing it has steam in it."[8]

The study of prophecy must produce the steam of productivity in the work of God. Unequivocally, the pursuit of prophecy in my life has made me a more passionate preacher and productive worker in the service of my Savior. The words of the Lord Jesus Christ ring in my ears: "I must work the works of him that sent me, while it is day: the night cometh, when no man can work." (John 9:4)

The Savior and Worship of God: The Problem of Indifference

One of the greatest profits or benefits from our study and application of Bible prophecy is that it focuses our lives on the Savior, the precious Son of God, and produces within our soul what A. P. Gibbs called the Christian's highest occupation—worship. This addresses the problem of indifference. It has been said that history is "His story." As we look through history in the light of Bible prophecy, we center on one Person, the Lord Jesus Christ; and as we focus on Him, we fall on our knees and worship Him.

The concept that worship must flow from our study of prophecy was heralded by Wiersbe when he said, "When worship and prophecy are divorced, the result is mere religious curiosity."[9]

On January 29, 1948, Jim Elliot, the soon-to-be missionary martyr at the hands of Auca Indians, wrote in his diary while studying Genesis 35,

> "Lord, I would recenter my spiritual life as Jacob does in this portion. Instead of Bethel he centers his experience on El-Bethel. Not the house of God, but the God of that house. Praise God, the Savior is exalted in heaven and there given His deserved place. As in earth, so in heaven. Even so come, Lord Jesus."[10]

Yes, the center of our worship is the God of the house of God. So it is not just prophecy but the key person spotlighted by prophecy, the

Lord Jesus Christ Himself, who calls us to worship. This becomes so clear as we read Revelation 19:10, "The testimony of Jesus is the spirit of prophecy."

Concerning this passage, John Walvoord says, "This means that prophecy at its very heart is designed to unfold the beauty and loveliness of our Lord and Savior Jesus Christ . . . Christ is not only the major theme of the Scriptures but also the central theme of prophecy."[11]

Concerning the importance of studying prophecy and its benefit of worship in the life of the believer, Charles Ryrie says, "It will help to make the unseen real and create within the believer's life the very atmosphere of heaven. One cannot do other than worship in reading the Revelation."[12]

A study of the book of Revelation should bring us to reverence the One who is the focus of Revelation, Jesus Christ Himself. Commenting on this truth, Gibbs states,

> "The remembrance feast points toward a time when the Lord shall return, for we eat the bread and drink the cup only till He comes. The great hope of the Church is the literal and personal coming again of the Lord Jesus Christ. It is a significant fact that about one sixth of the New Testament is taken up with this great event and its far-reaching consequences to the church, to Israel, and to the world. Throughout the vast, eternal ages, the redeemed shall worship the Lamb that was slain and liveth again."[13]

This causes us to sing the old hymn:

> "Lord of glory, we adore thee, Christ of God, ascended high. Heart and soul we bow before thee, glorious now beyond the sky. Thee we worship, Thee we praise, excellent in all thy ways. Lord of life, to death once subject, bless yet a curse once made of thy Father's heart the object, yet in depth the anguish laid. Thee we gaze on, thee we call, bearing here our sorrows all. Royal robes shall soon invest thee, royal splendors crown thy brow. Christ of God, our souls confess thee, king and

sovereign, even now. Thee we reverence, thee obey, own thee Lord in Christ always."[14]

The spotlight of prophecy turns to a future song of worship that the redeemed will sing around His throne. The words are as follows:

> "Thou art worthy to take the book, and to open the seals thereof: for thou wast slain, and hast redeemed us to God by the blood out of every kindred, and tongue, and people, and nation; and hast made us unto our God kings and priests: and we shall reign on the earth . . . Worthy is the Lamb that was slain to receive power, and riches, and wisdom, and strength, and honour, and glory, and blessing. (Revelation 5:9, 10, 12)

Wiersbe states,

> "Twenty-eight times in the book of Revelation, Jesus is referred to as the Lamb. The Greek word means a little pet lamb. The kind you would not want to see slain for any reason. The major themes of Revelation are all related to the Lamb. God's wrath is the wrath of the Lamb (6:16). The tribulation saints are washed in the blood of the Lamb (7:14). The story is consummated with the marriage of the Lamb (19:7) and the church is the Bride, the Lamb's wife (21:9). The heavenly throne is the throne of God and of the Lamb (22:1,3). Eliminate the Lamb and redemption from the Book of Revelation and there is very little left. We worship Him not only for who He is, and where He is, but also what He has done for us. The fact that He was slain indicates that He first took upon Himself a human body, for God as Spirit cannot die. When we worship the Lamb, we are bearing witness to the incarnation as well as the atonement."[15]

One of the great byproducts of a true worship of our Lord Jesus Christ is that it produces within our hearts a fervent desire to live a holy life for Him. In 2 Peter 3:11, the apostle Peter expresses it this way:

"Seeing then that all these things shall be dissolved, what manner of persons ought ye to be in all holy conversation and godliness."

Speaking to the fact of how true worship produces holy conduct, Scofield stated,

> "Let me say here that there is not such a thing as an abstract doctrine in Scripture. There is not a proposition of truth which is not intended by Almighty God to have an influence upon conduct. We know, and believe, and expect we shall be like Him when He shall appear; that we shall see Him as He is, and every man that hath this hope in Him purifieth himself even as He is pure."[16]

Yes, there can be much profit from studying prophecy. It addresses the whole problem of ignorance; increases our knowledge of the Scriptures, the Word of God; and enables us not only to have concepts but also clarity in God's program and plan for the ages. Also, it will address the problem of inactivity in the service and work of God. The true study of prophecy will motivate us to be actively involved in His work. Last, but not least, the proper study of prophecy will lead us to worship the central figure of all prophecy, the Lord Jesus Christ Himself. As you grow in your relationship with God and in your study of prophecy, may these words be used to enlighten you in His Word, to enlist you in His Work, and to enthrall you in His worship as we all bow before Him and sing with inflamed hearts of love, "Worthy is the Lamb that was slain, to receive power, and riches, and wisdom, and strength, and honor, and glory, and blessing." (Revelation 5:12)

Chapter Fourteen

Carry the Light

Excitement and euphoria filled the air as a splendidly prepared athlete approached the podium carrying the Olympic torch for his nation. The torch was passed, and the whole stadium exploded with cheers as the president of the International Olympic Committee announced, "Let the games begin!" This great opportunity was a tremendous reward for this young, well-conditioned athlete.

Watching this event unfold, I was reminded that, as believers in the Lord Jesus Christ, we have an even greater privilege and responsibility to carry the light of God. Listen to the words of the Spirit of God through the writer to the early Hebrew believers:

> "Wherefore seeing we also are compassed about with so great a cloud of witnesses, let us lay aside every weight, and the sin which doth so easily beset us, and let us run with patience the race that is set before us, looking unto Jesus the author and finisher of our faith; who for the joy that was set before him endured the cross, despising the shame, and is set down at the right hand of the throne of God." (Hebrews 12:1-2)

As we begin our study of "carrying the light," it is good to remember great men of God who have gone before us carrying the light.

John Bunyan, author of *Pilgrim's Progress*, was arrested for preaching the Gospel. While he was in prison, he was asked what he would do when released. His answer was, "Today as soon as I am released I will continue to preach the Gospel by the help of God."

As we consider this great privilege and responsibility, we must ask ourselves several questions: First, what is light, and what does it mean to carry the light? Then why carry the light, and where should I carry it? And finally, what can I learn from those in the past who have carried the light?

The Essence of Light

As we explore this awesome subject, let's start first with the essence of light. What is light? If we are to carry the light, what are we carrying?

Many times in the Scriptures, we see light as a figure of speech. In 1 John 1:5, it says, "God is light and in him is no darkness at all." Jesus Christ declared Himself to be the light of the world (John 8:12), and we know that the Word of God is light. (Psalm 119:105).

Let's consider the characteristics of light. Light attracts, but it also reveals or exposes that upon which it falls. Those who receive the Word of our Lord will be counted as light in the midst of darkness. Did you know it is impossible to hide light? For light penetrates the densest darkness (see John 1:5). Our Lord referred to this fact when He declared that a city located on a hilltop could not be hidden (Matthew 5:14). He also said that a lamp is not to be hidden under a bushel, but it should be placed where it could be seen and could illuminate everything around it (Matthew 5:15).

In the Jerusalem Temple, there was a great golden candelabrum which stood fifty cubits (seventy-three feet) high and was extremely beautiful. Every night this light was lit and shed its soft light across the whole city, reminding the people of the presence of God. Jesus, as He stood in that temple said, "I am the Light of the world . . ." (John 8:12), but to what was He referring? By this declaration, Jesus was really saying that He was the Messiah. Yes, Jesus Christ was the true sovereign of Israel, the Savior of the world.

Simeon, in Luke 2:32, refers to the Messiah as "a light to lighten the Gentiles and the glory of thy people Israel."

Just as the light in the sanctuary was always burning before the Lord, so Christ showed forth His light to the people of Israel and all around Him.

The light that Christ brought was the knowledge of the Father. That which He revealed about the Father through His life was not revealed in secret; for people do not light lamps to put them where the light will be hidden.

John 3:19 states, "Men loved darkness rather than light because their deeds were evil." This shows us the very essence of spiritual light and darkness. Light represents the knowledge of God and the life of God. Darkness represents ignorance of God and spiritual death before God. When we are carrying the light, we are manifesting the knowledge of God to those who are wrapped in darkness and the life of God to those who are dead in their trespasses and sins. This light is the very person of Jesus Christ, the light of the Word of God.

Notice carefully, we are not the light but, rather, those who reflect that light and prepare the way for the entrance of the True Light, Jesus Christ, and the knowledge of God Himself.

The Exhortation Concerning Light

Throughout the Scriptures, we see that God is Light and that Jesus Christ, the Son of God, declared Himself to be Light. God's Word is also called Light. But we see further that we are called to be reflectors of that light.

Remember that Jesus, in His great Sermon on the Mount, turned to His followers and said, "Ye are the light of the world." (Matthew 5:14) Then He went on to say, "Let your light so shine before men that they may see your good works and glorify your Father which is in heaven." (Matthew 5:16)

Very clearly, God called His first disciples to carry the light. They were to do it through their lives—that is, the testimony of what they were, and their lips—the testimony of what they said.

The exhortation is not only to show forth the knowledge of God in the way we live but also to share the great truth that Jesus Christ is the only One who can erase their ignorance of God through our words. We are to carry forth His message to this lost and dying world.

How marvelous are the words of our Lord to Paul and Barnabas in Acts 13:47, where we read, "Have set thee to be light of the Gentiles that thou shouldest be for salvation unto the ends of the earth."

Without a doubt, carrying the light was the plan of God for the apostle Paul's life. But here, I am reminded that it is not only the plan of God for the apostle Paul's life but also for your life and mine.

God's exhortation to you is to set your life in a place that it can be seen and, by your life and with your lips, show forth salvation to all those who are wrapped in darkness, those who are totally ignorant of God.

This is not your option; it is your obligation as you stand in your community, your school, your neighborhood, and even before your loved ones.

Those who are lost are wrapped in darkness and are totally ignorant of God's plan and need God's light. The exhortation to you today is to "carry that light."

The apostle Paul said that he was obedient to the heavenly vision (Acts 26:19). Are you obedient to God's command for your life? Do you know the Word of God well enough to show people who are wrapped in their own ignorance that Jesus Christ is the Way, the Truth, and the Life and that no man cometh to the Father but by Him? Do people see your life (good works) and glorify your Father who is in heaven? This exhortation is for you today.

Some may ask, is it possible to carry the light of the Gospel in public school today? I will remind you that with every command God gives us in His Holy Word, He equips us to carry out that command.

The Exercise of Carrying the Light

This brings us to the exercise of carrying the light. How do I go about it? How do I carry the light? Could I suggest a few ways that you might do this in your public school and neighborhood?

1. Carry your Bible: Thy Word is Light (see Psalm 119:105). During my last years of high school, I made a practice of placing my Bible on top of my books. The number of opportunities I had to speak up for Christ just as a result of carrying my Bible was unbelievable. Some students would pick up my Bible and say, "What is this? Are you a holy Joe or what?" At that point, I was able to share with them the truth of Jesus Christ and how He had changed my life. It was marvelous to see scores of them coming to Christ. You say we can't do that today in our society. What I

am telling you is that you have a First Amendment right, so do not cringe before the threats of men. Do what's right—Carry the light.

2. Through Gospel tracts: Find some good tracts that share the truth of salvation. Make sure they are full of Scripture and they are clear and relevant to the people whom you are seeking to touch for the glory of God.

3. Through a small cross or Jesus first pin that you can put on your coat or collar as a witnessing tool: People will ask you, "What is that?" At that point, you can share the truth of the Gospel of Christ. But remember, an effective witness cannot be sporadic, you must stay with it. As you are obedient to carry the light every single day in your school or workplace, God, in a marvelous way, will give you opportunities and open doors that you never dreamed possible. I know it works because, in my senior year of high school, over three hundred classmates came to Christ. Lives were touched for eternity because we simply obeyed the Word of God to carry forth the light. Here, you might say this was good for your generation, but I am reminded the Bible and the Gospel of Christ cut across generational lines, and God has no secret agents.

Enemies of Carrying the Light

The apostle Paul devoted his life to carrying the light to the whole Gentile world of his day. As he wrote his second letter to the believers at Corinth, Paul identified clearly the key enemy of carrying the light. Yes, you've got it—his name is Satan, Lucifer, the devil, that old serpent and dragon.

Listen to the words of the apostle Paul:

> "But if our Gospel be hid, it is hid to them that are lost: In whom the god of this world hath blinded the minds of them which believe not, lest the light of the glorious Gospel of Christ, who is the image of God, should shine unto them." (2 Corinthians 4:3, 4)

Unbelievable, but the chief enemy of carrying the light is called the god of this world. Satan is the ruler of this present age, and he carries out his devilish and destructive program by blinding the minds of those who do not believe. In an incredible way, he not only blinds the minds of those who do not believe, but he also tries to impede believers from carrying the light. He does this through planting doubts in your minds, diluting your motives, and—a big one—taking you to great detours in your manner of life.

Just think, when you doubt your own ability to carry the light, you are really doubting God's power and His promises to enable you to be His messenger. So the doubt is not in yourself, it is in God Himself, and Satan has accomplished his devilish scheme in your life.

Carrying the light is important, but we must also be sure of our motivation—to glorify God and see the salvation of souls. Many times Satan will delude our motives by trying to make us think that we are stars instead of servants. If our desire is to be a star, we will not want to say or do anything that will make people think less of us. Sometimes it is just a hidden desire to be popular or accepted in our school or neighborhoods. Peer pressure is just an excuse that is made because of the desire to have people like us instead of loving our Savior. Don't forget the apostle Paul said he was not ashamed of the Gospel of Christ. Are you?

If Satan cannot delude our motives through those means, he will try to get us on rabbit trails or detours, such as trying to promote a particular church or denomination or getting into religious arguments that lead only to division. Remember, it is possible to win an argument and lose a soul. We are not out to promote anyone, but Jesus Christ alone.

There are all types of causes that Christians get caught up with, and yet many of them fall so short of the main purpose in life: to carry the glorious Gospel of Christ to a world that lies in darkness. It is a tragedy, but often we become our own worst enemies by losing sight of the empowering Spirit of God in our lives and the explosive power of the Word of God. We sell ourselves short and also affect others by not carrying the light. What a tragedy to turn our backs for eternity on our friends who do not know Christ.

I was jolted with this truth some years ago as I came across a little poem titled "My Friend." Read carefully these words:

My friend, I stand in the judgment now
And I feel that you're to blame somehow.
On earth I walked with you day by day
And never once did you point the way.
Yes, I called you my friend in life
Trusted you through joy and strife.
And yet in coming to this terrible end
How can I call you, my friend?[1]

Examples to Follow

To help us not to fall into this horrible trap, we would do well to consider the examples of those who in the past have faithfully carried the light. Just as their generation was touched with the light of the Gospel of Christ, so our generation can be touched today.

First, I think of impulsive Peter, who came to the light through the testimony of his brother Andrew. The Scripture says of Andrew, "He first findeth his own brother Simon, and saith unto him, We have found the Messias, which is, being interpreted, the Christ." (John 1:41)

Yes, as Andrew passes off the scene, Peter is the key figure, not only in the Gospels, but also in the book of Acts. Peter was always the one speaking—up front, vocal, even impetuous—yet he became a light to his generation. He was willing to speak up, step up, and stand up for God. On the Day of Pentecost, it was Peter who shut the mouths of the mocking Jews and preached Jesus Christ as Savior and sovereign. This was the same Peter who cut off Malcus's ear, jumped into the water to swim to the shores of the Galilee as Jesus said, "Come and dine."

Impulsive, yes, but he was always ready to give an answer to those who asked for a reason of his faith. Maybe you are like Peter. May I challenge you to use all your energies for Christ?

Then I think of industrious Stephen. He was one who was called to wait upon tables. He was a "behind the scenes" kind of guy, caring for the needs of the believers in the early church. Stephen was faithful just doing the mundane task of waiting on tables. Yet this man truly knew the Scriptures and was filled with the Spirit of God. God used Stephen to give us the longest sermon in the book of Acts. Yet because of his message, Stephen was stoned to death, and during his lifetime, he saw no visible results. Nevertheless, he faithfully carried the light even unto death, and in eternity, Stephen will truly shine forth as a crown of God because of his faithfulness. Maybe you have a mundane task, and maybe you are hidden from the sight of others, yet God will use you in ways, places, and even at times you never dreamed of. It might even cost you your life, like Cassie Bernall in Columbine High School. Be a Stephen; be a crown of God, and carry the light.

The last example I see is that of intellectual Paul. Without a doubt, there is no one in all of the New Testament whom God used in a greater way than the apostle Paul. God used him to not only carry the light but also to reveal the mind of God through his writings.

God used this man to bring to us His great truths in written form. Paul was an intellectual giant in his day. Listen to his own personal testimony from Philippians 3:4-6:

> "Though I might also have confidence in the flesh. If any other man thinketh that he hath whereof he might trust in the flesh, I more: Circumcised the eighth day, of the stock of Israel, of the tribe of Benjamin, an Hebrew of the Hebrews; as touching the law, a Pharisee; concerning zeal, persecuting the church; touching the righteousness which is in the law, blameless."

What a resume! What credentials! But this would all be counted as nothing. The apostle Paul viewed everything he had received as a gift from God and would not be puffed up by his own human achievements. He goes on to say,

> "But what things were gain to me, those I counted loss for Christ. Yea doubtless, and I count all things but loss for the excellency of the knowledge of Christ Jesus my Lord: for whom I have suffered the loss of all things, and do count them but dung, that I may win Christ." (Philippians 3:7-8)

He would debate with the intellectuals of his day but never considered himself as someone special. Truly, the apostle Paul made himself as nothing so that God might glorify Himself through his life.

All these men and even more carried the light. Maybe you are like Peter, Stephen, or even Paul. Maybe you don't think that you have anything in common with these men. However, I would remind you that you do because God has planted within your heart His light: the light of the glorious Gospel. God has given you His Spirit, the very one that brings forth the ministry of illumination and regeneration. He has given you His infallible Word, the very light of God. Would you carry the light? Would you be encouraged to do so? The God who uses all types of vessels wants to use you to carry this light to your generation.

Jack Wyrtzen said it so well with these words: "I believe it is the responsibility of every generation to reach their generation for Christ." Jack did that his entire life, and now it is up to you and me to carry the light. It is an awesome privilege and a great responsibility, but God has enabled you. You have what it takes, so go for it. Carry that torch, and you too, as God's Olympic athlete, will arrive at the shores of Heaven rejoicing because you have been enabled by His Spirit to carry the light.

As we carry the light, we must remember that our Lord called us the light of the world (Matthew 5:14). To the measure that we take in the light of God in our lives will be the extent we can reflect that light to the world.

That light is the Scripture, the Son of God, and the Spirit of God. When I think of this world, I am reminded of the words of the apostle Paul in Philippians 2:15: "That ye may be blameless and harmless, the sons of God, without rebuke, in the midst of a crooked and perverse nation, among whom ye shine as lights in the world . . ."

Our ability to recognize darkness in this world system will be determined by the amount of light in our lives. Don't forget the world where we live is blind, and the only hope for them to see is our ability to carry the light.

Chapter Fifteen

I Pledge Allegiance: Understanding the Foundation of Biblical Commitment

"**I** pledge allegiance to the flag of the United States of America . . ." is a phrase most Americans gladly and proudly embrace because of love of country. In the midst of this pledge, the flag stands as a symbol for the believer, and it too is our banner representing the very foundation of all that we believe. In years past, Word of Life used a shield that incorporated a cross to identify their ministry. Upon that shield, our ministry banner as it were was the open Bible and the empty cross.

In this brief study, I want to challenge you to think with me about the words "I pledge allegiance."

In a day of open compromise and a total lack of loyalty, it is imperative to pledge allegiance. I am greatly offended by some athletes who refuse to stand for our national anthem, but even more so by those who refuse to show their open allegiance to an empty cross and an open Bible.

As you open the Scriptures, you will see again and again the servants of the Lord being dedicated to the service of the Lord. Leviticus 8 gives a detailed account of the priests being set apart for the service to which God had called them. These were the ones separated, the ones who would stand apart and carry out the service of the Lord. In this detailed dedication service, every aspect of their person and the work to which they were called was to be set apart unto the Lord. Notice the words of God, which Moses commanded to the sons of Aaron, who made up the priesthood:

"Therefore shall ye abide at the door of the tabernacle of the congregation day and night seven days, and keep the charge of the Lord, that ye die not: for so I am commanded." (Leviticus 8:35)

Keep the charge of the Lord. This phrase is very similar to our words, "I pledge allegiance." But what does it mean to say that we pledge allegiance?

Webster's dictionary defines a pledge as "a solemn promise or agreement; something delivered as security for the fulfillment of a promise." Both definitions contain the element of a promise that must be fulfilled.

As we think of the word "allegiance," again, we see from *Webster's Dictionary* that "allegiance" is "total absolute loyalty as to a government, a sovereign, a person, a group or a cause." In this light, to say "I pledge allegiance" is to make a solemn promise of absolute loyalty.

In our day, some are just starting to wake up to the fact that these words have only been mouthed but not meant. It is one thing to say the words but something quite different to live them out. But before we point our finger at those outside of the family of God, isn't it true that as believers often we say words like "I pledge allegiance to the Lamb," and yet at times they are just words devoid of any real sense of commitment?

As we consider our pledge of allegiance, I want to remind you that a pledge is a very solemn promise. Another way we might think of a pledge is to see it as a token of total, absolute loyalty. As you look in the Scriptures, you will see that the concept of a pledge was used in several different ways. Sometimes it was used in very sad situations, and sometimes it was even used in very shameful situations. For instance, do you remember that Tamar asked for a pledge from Judah? In Genesis 38: 17, we read her words, "What will you give me as a pledge?"

This is what Tamar asked as she entered into a sinful sexual relationship with her father-in-law, Judah. Tamar had disguised herself in such a way that Judah did not recognize her. The pledge he gave her was his signet or seal. This seal was on a cord that went around his neck, and he gave it to her, signifying that he would follow through on the price he had agreed to pay her. Later, after having sexual relations with Judah, Tamar kept the signet; and Judah was frantic to find out what had become of his pledge, his token.

Another example of a pledge is found in Exodus 22:26. There, we read of the taking of a neighbor's garment as a pledge. In this passage, careful instructions are written with directions to give back the pledge before nightfall. A similar concept is found in Deuteronomy 24:10-13, where we read, "If he is poor do not sleep with his pledge." The idea here is that the pledge was to be returned before the setting of the sun.

So what is a pledge? It is a solemn promise at times involving a token that would be forfeited if the one making the pledge did not fulfill their promise with regard to the pledge.

In a positive sense, it's interesting to note that the Holy Spirit Himself is given to believers as a pledge. I do not know of any greater basis for security of salvation. The Spirit of God being the pledge from God guarantees that God will fulfill His promise of salvation. And if not, the pledge would be lost, and that is totally out of the question. So a pledge is speaking of a very solemn promise ratified by a token given as a guarantee of the fulfillment of the promise made.

As Americans, we pledge our allegiance to the flag, but as believers, our allegiance is to our Lord. We abide as blood-bought, born-again citizens with an even higher calling. And when we say "Lord, I pledge to You my allegiance," we are, in effect, saying, "Lord, I'm going to keep the charge." The question for us today concerns how that works out practically in our daily lives.

Allegiance to the Will of God

To pledge allegiance to the Lord means I pledge allegiance to the will of God.

In Psalm 40:6-8, we read,

> "Sacrifice and offering thou didst not desire; mine ears hast thou opened: burnt offering and sin offering hast thou not required. Then said I, Lo, I come: in the volume of the book it is written of me, I delight to do thy will, O my God: yea, thy law is within my heart."

When the psalmist writes of opening his ears (v. 6), the allusion is to a practice explained in Exodus 21. There, we read that a servant could make a pledge by placing his ear on the doorpost of the city in the presence of his master. Then, upon the doorpost, the servant would take a sharp instrument and drive it through his own earlobe, marking himself as a bondslave for life. A bondslave chose to give up his right to freedom to serve his master. That concept caught the hearts and minds of the early believers. As you look into the epistles, you will see that Peter called himself a bondslave. John called himself a bondslave. James called himself a bondslave. And Judas, the half-brother of our Lord, called himself a bondslave.

Do you know what each of these men were saying? They were stating their allegiance to the will of God. It was no longer their will, but God's will that mattered. The Lord Jesus Christ expressed the same attitude when, in His most difficult hour, He said, "Not as I will, but as Thou will." (Matthew 26:39)

As we say "I pledge allegiance to the Lord," it means that we are pledging our allegiance to the will of God. Like the bondslave, we are saying, "Mark me, O God, that all may see that I no longer live for my will but Your will, Your will regarding what I do with my life and where I go, Your will regarding my life's partner and how I will live out my days . . . I pledge allegiance to the will of God."

Upon a quiet New England hill in Northfield, Massachusetts, rests the tombstone and burial site of D. L. Moody. His life verse, which is on that tombstone, reads, "And the world passeth away and the lust thereof, but he that doeth the will of God abideth forever." (1 John 2:17)

As he embraced this verse, Moody was saying that the lasting impact of a life is determined by a pledge to the will of God.

Romans 12:2 says that the will of God is good, acceptable, and perfect. Knowing that God is good and that His will for us is perfect, how foolish it would be to not stand up and be counted saying "I pledge allegiance to the will of God"?

Allegiance to the Word of God

Not only should we pledge our allegiance to the will of God, but we also should pledge our allegiance to the Word of God. The psalmist said, "Thy word is a lamp unto my feet, and a light unto my path." (Psalm 119:105) He also went on to say, "Thy word have I hid in mine heart, that I might not sin against thee." (Psalm 119:11)

Is the Word of God hidden in your heart? When we proclaim our allegiance to the Word of God, it is serious business. It means that when God speaks, I will obey. It means that the Word of God is my greatest delight. The psalmist wrote, "How sweet are thy words unto my taste! Yea, sweeter than honey to my mouth." (Psalm 119:103)

The apostle Paul said it this way when he wrote to young Timothy, "Study to show thyself approved unto God, a workman that needeth not to be ashamed, rightly dividing the word of truth." (2 Timothy 2:15)

I pledge allegiance to the Word of God means that I do not have a casual handling of the Word of God, nor do I have a curious handling of the Word of God; it is not just novelty. If I pledge my allegiance to the Word of God, then my handling of it will be constant, committed, and correct. The Word of God is our manual, our guide.

Jim Elliot, who gave his life in the service of Jesus Christ, was asked why he didn't stay in the United States. His reply was, "America is condemned by the balance of their checkbooks and the dust on their Bibles." He made that statement several years ago, but today the society in which we live is more biblically illiterate than ever before in the history of the church of our Lord Jesus Christ.

A pledge of allegiance to God means that I'm pledging allegiance to the will of God; no longer independently determining what I will do or where I will go. My mind and heart and all my being will be committed in total loyalty to the Word of God. But there is another aspect to this pledge, and that is I also pledge allegiance to the work of God.

Allegiance to the Work of God

The Lord Jesus in John 9:4 said, "I must work the work of him that sent me for the night cometh when no man can work."

I must work. I believe God has given us a window of time, and that window is quickly closing. Would we consider our pledge of allegiance in this way? I must. I must do the work that God has given me while the time is available, for the day will come when the opportunity will have passed and no longer will I be able to work and serve God as I now can.

Jesus, in His high-priestly prayer found in John 17:4, said, "I have finished the work that thou gavest me to do."

That too is my prayer, that I will be able to one day stand before the Lord and say that, by God's grace, I finished the work that He gave me to do. Is that possible? Yes, it is. The apostle Paul said it like this: "I have fought a good fight, I have finished my course I have kept the faith." (2 Timothy 4:7)

If you pledge your allegiance to the will of God, then you will be a marked person; you will be a bondslave and live no longer for your own will but for God's will; no longer will you be driven by what you want, but your motivation will come from what He wants. This will be fleshed out by a total commitment to the work of God.

At the beginning of this study, we noted the solemn words charged to those who would serve God, "Keep the charge." The charge was that of faithfulness. Years later, the apostle Paul said something similar to young Timothy. In 1 Timothy 5:21, he says, "I charge you before God, and the Lord Jesus Christ and the elect angels."

Paul gave him a charge. Again, we read, "But thou, O man of God, flee these things; and follow after righteousness, godliness, faith, love, patience, meekness. Fight the good fight of faith, lay hold on eternal life, whereunto thou art also called, and hast professed a good profession before many witnesses. I give thee charge in the sight of God, who quickeneth all things, and before Christ Jesus, who before Pontius Pilate witnessed a good confession." (1 Timothy 6:11-13)

And then in 2 Timothy, he wrote, "I charge thee therefore before God, and the Lord Jesus Christ, who shall judge the quick and the dead at his appearing and his kingdom; preach the word; be instant in season, out of season; reprove, rebuke, exhort with all long suffering and doctrine." (2 Timothy 4:1-2)

I pledge allegiance means I pledge allegiance to the will of God. I pledge allegiance to the Word of God, and I pledge allegiance to the work of God. I want to remind all of us that just as we saw at the beginning, it's a solemn promise with a token, and it speaks of absolute, total loyalty.

As God works in the hearts of men, He moves some to preach sermons and others He moves to write songs. Charles Wesley was reading a commentary written by Mathew Henry on the portion of Leviticus 8:35, which we looked at earlier. After reading this commentary, Wesley wrote the words to a great hymn called "A Charge to Keep":

A charge to keep I have,
a God to glorify,
a never-dying soul to save,
and fit it for the sky.

> To serve the present age,
> My calling to fulfill;
> O may it all my powers engage
> To do my Master's will!
> Arm me with jealous care,
> As in thy sight to live,
> And oh, thy servant, Lord,
> Prepare a strict account to give!

The third verse ends with "a strict account to give." I believe, for many years, we have been guilty of playing church in America. We have turned the church into a playground of entertainment. But God is shaking us to see that it is a battlefield of engagement. And just as Charles Wesley wrote, "all my powers engage." We too must invest every effort because we have a charge to keep.

I pledge allegiance—when you say those words, do you say them glibly, maybe not even thinking deeply about the words? I believe most of America would have to confess that we have done this regarding our flag and that for which it stands. As a church, wouldn't we too have to confess that often we have mouthed the words of our commitment to God, not realizing what it means to pledge allegiance to His will and to His Word and to His work? Have we engaged all our resources to keep our charge knowing that one day there will be a solemn accounting for it?

***

One of the most famous battles of the World War II was fought in France, on the beaches of Normandy. A few years ago, I was there and walked on those beaches. I stood on the cliffs and saw the bunkers and the craters were on that day the mortars fell. It was an unbelievable sight. There, sixty rangers led by Col. James Rutter scaled those heights through all the fighting and all the fire liberating France, then Europe, and then the world. Near this famous historic site is probably the most beautiful cemetery I have ever seen. There, thousands of little white crosses stand row upon row, symmetrically aligned. As I walked among those crosses, it was almost sunset, and in the distance, I heard taps being played. I turned toward the sound and saw the American flag. It was incredibly moving. There, among those crosses, is a wall inscribed with the names of over 1,557 soldiers who died for our freedom. On the top of that wall, I read these words: "To these we owe the high resolve that the cause for which they died we shall live!"

In the same way, many a brother and sister in Christ have given their lives in defense of religious freedoms which we enjoy, and it is the precious blood of our risen Savior that purchased our redemption. With this in mind, could we pledge anything less than our all?

I PLEDGE ALLEGIANCE!

Chapter Sixteen

The Anointing of the Holy Spirit

Perhaps no Bible doctrine is more misunderstood in the church today than the doctrine concerning the Holy Spirit of God. In relationship to the lack of understanding of the person and work of the Holy Spirit of God, the two main problems that plague the church today are the problems of apathy and ignorance. On one hand, certain so-called fundamental, orthodox Christians are so apathetic in their lifestyle that they show few evidences of the person and work of the Holy Spirit of God in their lives. On the other hand, some Christians with much zeal are totally entrenched in their ignorance. This ignorance is a lack of knowledge concerning the biblical teaching of the person and work of the Holy Spirit of God. Much of this problem of ignorance exists because teaching has gone through the faulty funnel of Christian experience instead of finding its basis in sound biblical exegesis.

Before we discuss the important subject of the anointing of the Holy Spirit, we need to consider for a moment the baptism of the Holy Spirit. The prevailing confusion in the treatment of this doctrine has risen from many factors. The principal cause of disagreement is found in a common failure to understand the distinctive nature of the church. Many theologians regard the church as the universal group of saints from every age of human history.

Dr. John Walvoord, in his classic work on the Holy Spirit of God, states, "If this concept of the nature of the Church is held, the Baptism of the Holy Spirit has no relation to it. As this ministry is not found in the Old Testament, it is not included in any prophecies regarding the Millennium, it is peculiarly the work of the Holy Spirit for the present age, beginning with Pentecost and ending at the Resurrection of the righteous when the Living Church is translated. If, however, the Church be defined as the saints of this age only, the work of the Holy Spirit in baptizing all true believers into the Body of Christ takes on a new meaning. It becomes the distinguishing mark of the saints of the present age, the secret of the peculiar intimacy and relationship of Christians to the Lord Jesus Christ. It is, therefore, essential to a proper doctrine of the baptism of the Holy Spirit that it be recognized as the distinguishing characteristic of the Church, the body of Christ."[1]

Because of this truth, we clearly state the following:

The Baptism of the Holy Spirit Is

A. Only for the church age
B. Universal among all church age believers
C. A positional truth, not an experiential one
D. An instantaneous act at the moment of belief in Christ, not a repeated action

A careful study of the major passage concerning the baptismal work of the Holy Spirit of God (1 Corinthians 12:13) will give a basis of interpretation for all other passages.

Having laid this foundation, let us move on to discuss the misunderstanding concerning the anointing or the unction of the Holy Spirit.

The Holy Spirit's anointing is taken by many to be a post-salvation experience: one that gives the Christian special power in areas of ministry.

Today many prominent charismatic teachers have saturated the Christian public with errant teaching concerning the anointing of God's Spirit, which they claim is evidenced by being "slain in the Spirit" and even being "drunk in the Spirit." This teaching leads Christians to pursue extra-biblical and anti-biblical experiences. In this study, it will be our purpose to examine what the Bible teaches concerning the Holy Spirit's anointing and then determine its application to the Christian life.

A Biblical Definition

The word for "anoint" in the Greek text is *chrio*. Although the simple root word only occurs five times in the New Testament, it occupies a prominent place in all the Bible. We can see this, for instance, in how Israel marked its special men for God's service. There is the anointing of prophet, priest, and king. All these anointings seem to have initiated their special service for God.

In the New Testament, the idea of anointing takes on a special meaning. The word "Christ" is derived from the Greek verb *chrio*, which means "to anoint." This means that when Jesus of Nazareth is called Christ, He is identified as the "Anointed One." This form of the word "anoint" appears 529 times in the New Testament. It is the New Testament equivalent to the Old Testament word "Messiah." The Holy Spirit descending on Him at His baptism was the public manifestation of this anointing.

Its Biblical Usage

As we previously stated, three office-bearers in Israel were anointed: prophet, priest, and king.

Let's take a look at those.

A. The Prophet

In 1 Kings 19:16, we see that Elisha was to be anointed to be a prophet.

B. The Priest

At the birth of the Levitical priesthood, the service of recognition and consecration was characterized by anointing. (Exodus 29:29; Leviticus 14:3, 5).

C. The King

Samuel anointed Saul and David to be the first kings over God's people, Israel. When Samuel set out to select a king for Israel, he took along the anointing oil. (1 Samuel 16:1-13)

All these three concepts—prophet, priest, and king—find their culmination in the Messiah. Messiah means the "Anointed One" (Psalm 2:2; Isaiah 61:1, 2). His name, "Messiah" or the "Anointed One," is carried over into the New Testament, especially into the writings of Luke. Luke, in his Gospel, quotes directly the prophecy from Isaiah (Luke 4:18; Isaiah 61:1, 2); and in Acts, Jesus is called the Anointed One (Acts 4:26, 27; 10:38).

Biblical Understanding and Application

The key verses that have caused many problems with interpretation are found in 1 John 2:20, 27.

These verses say, "But ye have an unction from the Holy One, and ye know all things." (v. 20)

"But the anointing which ye have received of him abideth in you, and ye need not that any man teach you: but as the same anointing teacheth you of all things, and is truth, and is no lie, and even as it hath taught you, ye shall abide in him." (v. 27)

To be able to understand these verses, we need to keep in mind the immediate context. John was dealing directly with the concept of the anti-Christ and false teachers. These false teachers were claiming to be recipients of special revelation from God. Some even think they may have referred to their special insight, as anointing. Later on, the Gnostics, another very similar sect to the one that was attacking the believers to which the apostle John wrote, did use this type of terminology. What is interesting is that while they were saying they had a special revelation or insight, at the same time, they were denying the very Deity of Christ.

As we look at these passages, we should ask ourselves the following questions:

1. What is the Unction or the Anointing?
2. Who has the Unction or the Anointing?
3. When does one receive the Unction or the Anointing?

1. What Is the Anointing?

The Anointing is no doubt the Holy Spirit of God since according to 1 John 2:27, the Anointing teaches. This clearly suggests that the Anointing is a Person and not an experience. The Holy Spirit of God who indwells each believer has a special ministry to teach us concerning the Person of Christ.

2. Who Has the Anointing?

It seems very clear that the Anointing is given to all Christians because all Christians receive the Holy Spirit of God at the moment of belief. This reception of the Holy Spirit of God is commonly called the indwelling of the Holy Spirit of God and is an evidence of salvation. We read very clearly in Romans 8:9, "Now if any man have not the Spirit of Christ, he is none of his."

If the Holy Spirit is the Anointing or the Unction, then all Christians must have the Anointing because those without the Holy Spirit are apart from Christ.

3. When Does the Anointing Occur?

In John 14:16, 17, Jesus promised that He would pray to the Father that He would give another Comforter and that this Comforter would abide with us forever. We see that this Comforter would not only dwell with us, but He would also dwell in us. The sending of the Holy Spirit of God in this new way (to abide within every Christian on a permanent basis) saw its first fulfillment on the Day of Pentecost, which marks the birth of the church. Since the Day of Pentecost, every believer at the moment of belief is both baptized into the body of Christ and, at the same time, given the Holy Spirit of God as a permanent resident.

Again, Dr. John Walvoord states, "A careful study of the seven references to the Anointing of the Holy Spirit (Luke 4:18; Acts 4:27; 10:38; 2 Corinthians 1:21; 1 John 2:20, 27, twice) will reveal that every use of anoint in relation to the Holy Spirit may be safely interpreted as the initial act of indwelling. The word, anoint, is used in the sense of apply and is essentially appropriate in view of the fact that oil is used as a type of the Spirit. The presence of the Spirit is the result of the anointing, and every reference to anointing by the Spirit is used in this sense."[2]

Application

So what can we say about the anointing of the Holy Spirit of God in reference to the life of each believer? As we have looked at 1 John 2:20, 27, these verses seem to indicate that the anointing of the Holy Spirit is the very Spirit of God indwelling the believer as a teacher. In the context of 1 John 2, this teaching has special application concerning the Person of Christ. The Holy Spirit of Christ who indwells each believer has a special ministry to teach us concerning the Person of Christ. This was prophesied by Christ Himself when He said, "But the Comforter, which is the Holy Ghost, whom the Father will send in my name, he shall teach you all things, and bring all things to your remembrance, whatsoever I have said unto you." (John 14:26)

It is also interesting to note that Christ called the Holy Spirit "the Spirit of truth" in John 14:17. The Holy Spirit, which is our anointing or unction, surely leads us to understand the truth because He is the Spirit of Truth, and He helps us distinguish between truth and error.

Furthermore, Christ said, "Howbeit when he, the Spirit of truth, is come, he will guide you into all truth." (John 16:13)

Just as the anointing in the Old Testament enabled the prophet, priest and king to commence and carry out their special function, so the Holy Spirit of God, our Anointing, enables us to understand God's truth. For this reason, we do not need to pray for special unction or anointing on our ministry, seeing that we already have that Unction and Anointing in the Holy Spirit of God.

Then what should our prayer be? Our prayer should be centered on the controlling ministry of the Holy Spirit of God. Ephesians 5:18 says clearly that we are to be continually filled or controlled by the Holy Spirit of God. The filling or the controlling ministry of the Spirit of God (the same Holy Spirit that indwells us, the same Holy Spirit that is our unction or our anointing) unleashes all His power to carry out every aspect of life and ministry for the glory of the head of the church, our Lord Jesus Christ.

May we be diligent to allow the Holy Spirit of God to control our lives by living in a constant place of obedience and submission to God's work within us.

Chapter Seventeen

Teach Me to Pray: How Prayer Changes Things

Over the years, I have had occasion to speak in private with many successful Christian leaders. Invariably, as we compare notes and discuss the challenges of our busy lives, many of these men will share their wish that they could spend more time in prayer.

If you have listened to many missionary stories or read the biographies of successful Christian leaders, you will note an emphasis on prayer and probably have heard some amazing stories of God answering prayer; in some cases, just in the nick of time or to the exact dollar amount needed in a crisis.

Missionary Hudson Taylor of the famous China Inland Mission tells in his autobiography of preparing for a life of trusting God by not even asking his employer for the money due him at the end of the week, preferring instead to pray for the absent-minded individual to give it. One week his employer, a medical doctor, left the office on Friday without paying young Hudson. Hudson went home to find his landlord at his door demanding rent payment. Hudson prayed. The doctor was called back to his office in a medical emergency and, while there, remembered that he had forgotten to pay Hudson and rectified the oversight before leaving.

Asking and receiving is only one aspect of prayer. Unfortunately, it is the aspect that gets the most attention because we naturally are concerned with our pressing needs and are quick to ask God to help us. Jesus left for us an amazing example. Here was God in the flesh. Technically, He needed nothing. Whatever He wanted, He could have produced by His own power as God; nor did He need guidance. However, in His life, we see Him regularly seeking out privacy to fellowship with His heavenly Father. The night before He chose His twelve disciples, He spent the night in prayer. If the Son of God wanted to pray and benefitted from prayer and in His existence as a human needed prayer, certainly, we should be interested in prayer.

Another touching prayer factor is seen in the New Testament. The Gospel writers tell us that in Jesus's public ministry, His own brothers did not believe Him, nor did they encourage Him. However, once He had died and resurrected, several (if not all) became believers. His brother James was a key leader in the church in Jerusalem and wrote the epistle of James. In church history, James had a nickname, Old Camel Knees. Apparently, he spent so much time on his knees praying to the brother he shunned in life that they became obviously calloused, just like camels' knees. Interestingly enough, in his epistle, when James wanted to talk about the power of the prophet Elijah, he did not report on any of his miracles, such as raising the widow's son back to life (1 Kings 17:22), but rather the power that Elijah experienced in prayer. (1 Kings 17:1; 18:41).

> "The effectual fervent prayer of a righteous man availeth much. Elijah was a man subject to like passions as we are, and he prayed earnestly that it might not rain: and it rained not on the earth by the space of three years and six months. And he prayed again, and the heaven gave rain, and the earth brought forth her fruit." (James 5:16-18)

If we then are to be men and women of prayer, what should our prayer life look like?

Taking all the Scripture that relates to the matter, there seems to be four major aspects necessary in a human's prayer walk with God. Actually, all four of these aspects are illustrated in the model prayer that Jesus gave to His disciples when they said, "Lord, teach us to pray."

> "And it came to pass, that, as He was praying in a certain place, when he ceased, one of his disciples said unto him. Lord, teach us to pray, as John also taught his disciples. And he said unto them, When ye pray, say,

> *Our Father which art in heaven,*
> *Hallowed be thy name.*
> *Thy kingdom come.*
> *Thy will be done, as in heaven, so in earth.*
> *Give us day by day our daily bread.*
> *And forgive us our sins; for we also forgive every one that is indebted to us.*
> *And lead us not into temptation;*
> *but deliver us from evil."* (Luke 11:1-4)

The four ingredients are "adoration," "confession," "thanksgiving," and "supplication." The first letters of each word produce an easy to remember acronym: ACTS.

Adoration: Psalm 22:1-4

God is a great God and is worthy to be praised. He requests that we respect and honor Him. A human would be considered proud and even arrogant to make such requests, but because God is perfect, He is absolutely right to conclude that such perfection is worthy of praise. We struggle with the concept of "worship." There are all kinds of ideas of what real worship involves. Many insist it has to include music. Others look for outpourings of emotions. Some think it involves repetitive rituals and ceremonial acts. While it can include all these, the root idea is that of expressing respect. Some of the biblical words for worship have the root idea of "to kiss." Our English word "worship" comes from the Old English word "worthship." It means that we are describing the "worth" of the object of our attention.

The way to do that with God is by meditating on His names and attributes. His many names are descriptive of what He wants to be or do for us, and His attributes speak of the power He has to do so. For instance, one of His names is Jehovah Sabbaoth. "Sabbaoth" is the word for "hosts" or "armies." It refers to the angels of heaven, which form His army. God has ample military power to accomplish His tasks on earth. A parallel attribute would be "omnipotence," which means "all powerful."

Therefore, when we say to "praise the name of Jesus," we are not saying shout out the name Jesus, nor are we saying think of how Jesus is spelled—J, E, S, U, S. Rather, we are saying think about what the name

"Jesus" means ("Jehovah Saves") and meditate on the character qualities of the Godman Jesus who is able to save.

Psalm 22:1-4 is a powerful invitation for humans to adore our Creator God:

> *My God, my God, why hast thou forsaken me?*
> *Why art thou so far from helping me, and from the words of my roaring?*
> *O my God, I cry in the daytime, but thou hearest not;*
> *and in the night season, and am not silent.*
> *But thou art holy,*
> *O thou that inhabitest the praises of Israel.*

Psalm 22:1 is a prophetic word indicating what Christ would say on the cross. Therefore, we could say that verse 3 is not just David's idea, but Christ's conviction as well: "God inhabits the praise of His people!"

Do you want to be near the place where God lives? Adore Him, praise Him, and there He is—not just visiting but "inhabiting." Another thought is very convicting to me. In the Old Testament, we have descriptions and accounts of the complicated and expensive ceremonies involved in worshipping God with many sacrifices paid for by the people. Because of the cross of Christ, we do not have to pay for or bring any animal sacrifices. With that in mind, however, the author of the letter to the Hebrews challenges church age believers:

"We have an altar, whereof they have no right to eat which serve the tabernacle. For the bodies of those beasts, whose blood is brought into the sanctuary by the high priest for sin, are burned without the camp. Wherefore Jesus also, that he might sanctify, the people with his own blood, suffered without the gate. Let us go forth therefore unto him without the camp, bearing his reproach. For here have we no continuing city, but we seek one to come. By him therefore let us offer the sacrifice of praise to God continually, that is, the fruit of our lips, giving thanks to his name." (Hebrews 13:10--15)

Let us offer the sacrifice of praise.

Confession: 1 John 1:9

The second aspect of prayer in Scripture involves how sin affects our prayer life.

In Psalm 66, David has four "paragraphs" of information (marked off by a concluding word "Selah" or "Think on this"). Here's the fourth and final section:

> *Come and hear, all ye that fear God,*
> *and I will declare what he hath done for my soul.*
>
> *I cried unto him with my mouth,*
> *and he was extolled with my tongue.*
>
> *If I regard iniquity in my heart,*
> *the Lord will not hear me:*
>
> *but verily God hath heard me;*
> *he hath attended to the voice of my prayer.*
>
> *Blessed be God,*
> *which hath not turned away my prayer,*
> *nor his mercy from me. (Psalm 66:16-20)*

Note that David understands that God will not "hear" the prayer of the sinner even though God is omniscient, knowing all things actual and possible. This means that He will not regard it, He will not respect it, and therefore, He will not answer it. Isaiah agrees,

> "Behold, the LORD'S hand is not shortened, that
> it cannot save; neither his ear heavy, that it cannot hear:
> But your iniquities have separated between you and your
> God, and your sins have hid his face from you, that he
> will not hear." (Isaiah 59:1-2).

The only prayer that God will "hear" from someone living in sin is a request to be forgiven for that sinful behavior.

In the case of a believer, the request for forgiveness is not to have that sin removed from their account or "washed away." That has already been accomplished at the cross of Christ and applied to our personal accounts at the moment of saving faith. It is, however, necessary for the restoration of fellowship, which is broken by our rebellion when we return to sinful ways.

A classic expression of this process in found in 1 John 1:9: "If we confess our sins, he is faithful and just to forgive us our sins, and to cleanse us from all unrighteousness."

The Greek word translated as "confess" means "to say the same thing." As a child, we crawl up in our daddy's lap and agree with him against ourselves. We admit that what we did, said, or thought was wrong and ask for his forgiveness and the restoration of our fellowship.

Most of the Western world has been riveted on the space program for the last sixty years. Man has such a fragile body that special precautions have to be taken when he goes into the vacuum of outer space. He must have the right oxygen mix to breathe and the right temperature and the right pressure. Millions of dollars have been spent in developing the space suits designed to protect the astronauts when they do their space walks.

This world is not our home. It is controlled by Satan. The world, the flesh, and the devil seek to destroy our spiritual lives. We are pilgrims passing through. Fortunately, God provides a spiritual "space suit" to protect our fragile spiritual lives. As we breathe in, we receive the oxygen of heaven. That would be like receiving information and encouragement from God as we read His Word daily. When we breathe out, we send our needs heavenward. We do this in prayer. When sin enters the picture, it is like stones clogging the pipeline to heaven. God's blessings don't come down, and our prayers don't go up. We can sense them bouncing off the ceiling. We begin to strangle spiritually.

That is when we need the 1 John 1:9 experience to make things right with God, restore our fellowship, and be able to "breathe in and breathe out" once again.

Thanksgiving: Hebrews 13:15

The Bible views our relationship with God as a "father/son" relationship. We are "born" into the family of God as "babes." We are treated like precious "children," and we also have the privilege of the official standing as "adult sons" in the family of God, with all the rights and responsibilities of "sons and daughters of the king."

Human parents delight in giving things to their children; however, they also expect the child to acknowledge the gift with a polite "thank you." Our Heavenly Father is no different and delights to be told of our appreciation when He answers our prayers.

An emphasis on being grateful and expressing that in verbal thanksgiving is scattered throughout the Bible. When Zerubbabel, Haggai, Zechariah, and Joshua the High Priest returned from the Babylonian Captivity with almost fifty thousand fellow Jews and laid the foundation for the new temple, note their heart attitude:

> "And they sang together by course in praising and giving thanks unto the LORD; because he is good, for his mercy endureth for ever toward Israel. And all the people shouted with a great shout, when they praised the LORD, because the foundation of the house of the LORD was laid." (Ezra 3:11)

When Jesus healed ten men of that hideous and despised disease of leprosy, only one man came back to thank Him, and Jesus had kind words for his gratefulness:

> "And it came to pass, as he went to Jerusalem, that he passed through the midst of Samaria and Galilee. And as he entered into a certain village, there met him ten men that were lepers, which stood afar off and they lifted up their voices, and said, Jesus, Master, have mercy on us. And when he saw them, he said unto them, Go show yourselves unto the priests. And it came to pass, that, as they went, they were cleansed. And one of them, when he saw that he was healed, turned back and with a loud voice glorified God, and fell down on his face at his feet, giving him thanks: and he was a Samaritan. And Jesus answering said, Were there not ten cleansed? but where are the nine? There are not found that returned to give glory to God, save this stranger. And he said unto him, Arise, go thy way: thy faith hath made thee whole." (Luke 17:11-19)

In Paul's discussion of the marks of a Spirit-filled life, "thankfulness" is one of the top three indicators:

> "And be not drunk with wine, wherein is excess; but be filled with the Spirit; speaking to yourselves in psalms and hymns and spiritual songs, singing and making melody in your heart to the Lord; giving thanks always for all things unto God and the Father in the name of our Lord Jesus Christ; submitting yourselves one to another in the fear of God." (Ephesians 5:18-21)

The author of Hebrews emphasizes that Christians still have a sacrifice to give even though we are excused from the expensive bloody animal sacrifices:

> "By him therefore let us offer the sacrifice of praise to God continually, that is, the fruit of our lips giving thanks to his name." (Hebrews 13:15)

The mark, therefore, of a child of God who has learned the value and ways of prayer is that no one ever has to say to him "What do you say?" when something is done for him. "Thank you" is always on his lips.!

Supplication: Romans 8:26-28

The fourth aspect of prayer in Scripture is that of "supplication." This is what we normally think of when we hear the word "prayer"— the idea that we are asking for something. This does not have to be selfish, however. We are commanded to pray for the welfare of others, and so a large part of our "supplication" can be "intercession" for others. We should be praying for those who we are directly responsible for, such as our family, neighbors, and co-workers. We should be praying for the lost that we would have an opportunity to share the Lord with them. We should pray for our believing friends that they might progress in their walk with the Lord.

One of the tragedies of Christian work is that we have a tendency to get so busy in the Lord's work that we forget the Lord. It has been said that "activity" is the "anesthetic" of many a believer's life. Our "can do" attitudes are a subtle reminder of our ego, pride, and tendency to religiosity that says "I can do it myself!" We can't save ourselves, we can't live holy lives in our own energy, and we can't serve in our own power. From start to finish, our spiritual life has to be energized by the power of God. Prayer is the way we plug into that power.

We often admire the speaking ability of the great preachers, evangelists, and missionaries of past revivals. One often overlooked fact is that most of these great outpourings of revival were preceded and nurtured by extensive periods of prayer. One notable example is the famous "Hay Stack Prayer Meeting" that is considered to be the fountainhead of the entire missionary movement of the nineteenth, twentieth, and twenty-first centuries. In 1806, five young college students in New England were impressed that they should meet for prayer for world evangelization. Originally intending to pray in an open field, a summer thunderstorm drove them to the shelter of a haystack where the windows of heaven opened the spiritual rains of world evangelization.

There are two key words in the Greek language for the concept of "supplication." One has the idea of waving an olive branch as you approach a person to make your request. Hebrews 5:7-8 illustrates this usage in the prayer life of Jesus Christ:

> "Who in the days of his flesh, when he had offered up prayers and supplications with strong crying and tears unto him that was able to save him from death, and was heard in that he feared; Though he were a Son, yet learned he obedience by the things which he suffered."

The second word occurs twice in Romans 8:26-27:

> "Likewise the Spirit also helpeth our infirmities: for we know not what we should pray for as we ought: but the Spirit itself maketh intercession for us with groanings which cannot be uttered And he that searcheth the hearts knoweth what is the mind of the Spirit, because he maketh intercession for the saints according to the will of God."

"Maketh intercession" is the English translation. The root verb has the idea of running to catch up with a person in order to walk side by side so you can have a polite conversation in which to make your request. Notice that not only are believers encouraged to approach God in this manner, but we are also told that when our words fail, the Holy Spirit will be our interpreter so we have the confidence that the requests are properly relayed to the Heavenly Father.

Let's review. The four major ingredients of the believers' prayers are

1. Adoration
2. Confession
3. Thanksgiving
4. Supplication

Are there any other issues to consider? I believe that there are. I would consider these to be the required attitudes and conditions of the one praying in order to receive answers to his prayers.

Requirements

First is the issue of "clean hands." In Psalm 24:1-4, David declares,
The earth is the LORD's, and the fulness thereof;
the world, and they that dwell therein.

For he hath founded it upon the seas,
and established it upon the floods.

Who shall ascend into the hill of the LORD?
Or who shall stand in his holy place?

He that hath clean hands, and a pure heart;
who hath not lifted up his soul unto vanity,
nor sworn deceitfully.

The second issue is the matter of our zeal. Hebrews 11:6 points out, "But without faith it is impossible to please him: for he that cometh to God must believe that he is, and that he is a rewarder of them that diligently seek him."

If we expect God to answer our prayers, there needs to be a level of intensity on our part. "God, bless the missionaries" is not going to accomplish anything. We must know the specifics of the needs, feel the tug at the heart, enter into their struggles, and speak passionately to the Lord about His available supply and the timing of His perfect plan for their situation.

The third issue is God's will. This is crucial for us to understand so we don't become discouraged. We particularly can become discouraged if we read some of the prayer promises in the Gospels in isolation. By themselves, some of these promises seem to say "Whatever you pray for, I will give you." We should intuitively know that this can't be the case because we are not wise enough to safely use such a blanket promise. Most of us would certainly misuse such a power. On the other hand, if we mistakenly think that this is how prayer works today and we pray diligently for the healing of a loved one and they die of cancer anyway, our confidence in God and His Word can be damaged. What we need to understand is that all prayer promises in the Bible are qualified by "God's will." In 1 John 5:14-15, it is made this emphatically clear:

> "And this is the confidence that we have in him, that, if we ask any thing according to his will, he heareth us: and if we know that he hear us, whatsoever we ask, we know that we have the petitions that we desired of him."

God only answers prayers that coincide with His will. Therefore, if, for His greater purposes, He wills a twenty-year-old to die prematurely of cancer, no amount of praying on our part can alter that outcome. This does not destroy the power or the purpose of prayer, however. Prayer is not for me to change events. Prayer is to change me. I pray, not to change God's will but to find God's will. God's will does not just determine the ends, but it determines all the steps to the ends as well. Therefore, if it is God's will that the person be healed of cancer, my prayers will be part of that process. If it is not His will to heal that person, my prayers will make me more sensitive to his sufferings and the needs of his family so I can be more of a comfort in their time of distress. Therefore, if I want to see positive answers to prayer, I must become thoroughly immersed in information about God and His will. The more accurately that I can discern His will, and then pray that His will be done, the higher the percentage of my prayers will be positively answered. Since I am not omniscient, I, therefore, must also accept the fact that some answers will be "yes," some will be "no, never," and some will be "not now, maybe later."

A fourth consideration is the glory of God. In 1 Samuel 12:22, Samuel explains why God will not forsake His promises to Israel: "For the LORD will not forsake his people for his great name's sake: because it hath pleased the LORD to make you his people."

Since God delights in bringing glory to Himself, we should be thinking of ways that we can do that and then pray for what we need to bring glory to Him.

For instance, let's say that your vehicle dies. You begin to pray for a replacement. As you pray, you are reminded that God owns the cattle on a thousand hills and the wealth in every mine. So you conclude the value of the replacement vehicle is immaterial to God's bankbook. So you eye up a nice Corvette sports car. It is pricey and expensive to maintain. It holds two people and little more. What are the odds that God would answer your prayer and send you this sports car as opposed to, say, praying for a fifteen-passenger van that would help transport the youth group to their activities? Which answer to prayer would bring more "glory to God"?

In conclusion, let me share some verses that either speak to or are supports for a strong (and this means time-intensive) prayer life.

1. Finding God's will one step and one day at a time

"Thy word is a lamp unto my feet, and a light unto my path." (Psalm 119:105)

"Trust in the LORD with all thine heart; and lean not unto thine own understanding. In all thy ways acknowledge him, and he shall direct thy paths." (Proverbs 3:5-6)

2. Confidence that God wants the very best for our lives

"For I know the thoughts I think toward you says the Lord, thoughts of peace and not of evil, to give you a future and a hope." (Jeremiah 29:11)

"Call unto me, and I will answer thee, and show thee great and mighty things, which thou knowest not." (Jeremiah 33:3)

"Ask, and it shall be given you; seek, and ye shall find; knock, and it shall be opened unto you: For every one that asketh receiveth; and he that seeketh findeth; and to him that knocketh it shall be opened. Or what man is there of you, whom if his son ask bread, will he give him a stone? Or if he ask a fish, will he give him a serpent? If ye then, being evil, know how to give good gifts unto your children, how much more shall your Father which is in heaven give good things to them that ask him?" (Matthew 7:7-11)

3. Vain repetition is useless but thoughtful repetition has a place

"And he spoke a parable unto them [to this end], that men ought always to pray, and not to faint . . . And he would not for a while: but afterward he said within himself Though I fear not God, nor regard man; Yet because this widow troubleth me, I will avenge her, lest by her continual coining she weary me . . . And shall not God avenge his own elect, which cry day and night unto him, though he bear long with them? I tell you that he will avenge them speedily. Nevertheless when the Son of man cometh, shall he find faith on the earth?" (Luke 18:1-8)

4. Raising dead bodies back to life is great, but we can pray for greater miracles—being part of the process of seeing dead spirits be born again

"Verily, verily, I say unto you, He that believeth on me, the works that I do shall he do also; and greater works than these shall he do; because I go unto my Father. And whatsoever ye shall ask in my name, that will I do, that the Father may be glorified in the Son. If ye shall ask any thing in my name, I will do it." (John 14:12-14).

5. Every prayer has at least one guaranteed positive answer— peace of mind

"Be careful for nothing; but in every thing by prayer and supplication with thanksgiving let your requests be made known unto God. And the peace of God, which passeth all understanding, shall keep your hearts and minds through Christ Jesus." (Philippians 4:6, 7)

6. We don't have to be smart, wise, or shrewd to pray effectively. We can even pray for help to pray.

"If any of you lack wisdom, let him ask of God, that giveth to all [men] liberally, and upbraideth not; and it shall be given him. But let him ask in faith, nothing wavering. For he that wavereth is like a wave of the sea driven with the wind and tossed." (James 1:5-6)

For some people, prayer is just mouthing words, but it should be not that. It should be our wonderful privilege and practice to commune with our precious Lord. We read in Exodus 33:11, "And the Lord spake unto Moses face to face, as a man speaketh unto his friend."

An Irish preacher, Joseph Scriven, in a moment of great personal pain, wrote these words which later became the beloved hymn" What a Friend We Have in Jesus."

Are we weak and heavy-leaden
Cumbered with a load of care?
Precious Savior still our refuge
Take it to the Lord in prayer
Can we find a friend so faithful
Who will all our burdens share?
Jesus knows our every weakness;
Take it to the Lord in prayer.

My dear friend, prayer is about talking to One who loves you and gave Himself for you.
TALK TO HIM TODAY!

Chapter Eighteen

Touched by the Angel: How the Touch of God Can Change Your Life

Setting the Stage

A few years ago, there was a popular television program called *Touched by an Angel*. Have you ever been touched by an angel? In the Bible, we read of a man who truly was touched by an angel. This touch was different from what most people would think and certainly different from what you would see on the small screen, but this touch changed his life. His name was Jacob, and we read about him in Genesis 32.

> "And Jacob went on his way, and the angels of God met him. And when Jacob saw them, he said, This is God's host: and he called the name of that place Mahana'im. And Jacob sent messengers before him to Esau his brother unto the land of Se'ir, the country of Edom." (Genesis 32:1-3)

Also in the latter part of chapter 32, we read,

> "And Jacob was left alone; and there wrestled a man with him until the breaking of the day. And when he saw that he prevailed not against him, he touched the hollow of his thigh; and the hollow of Jacob's thigh was out of joint, as he wrestled with him. And he said, Let me go, for the day breaketh. And he said, I will not let thee go,

except thou bless me. And he said unto him, What is thy name? And he said, Jacob. And he said, Thy name shall be called no more Jacob, but Israel: for as a prince hast thou power with God and with men, and host prevailed. And Jacob asked him, and said, Tell me, I pray thee, thy name. And he said, Wherefore is it that thou dost ask after my name? And he blessed him there. And Jacob called the name of the place Peni'el: for I have seen God face to face, and my life is preserved." (Genesis 32:24-30)

Now he was touched by an angel.

Today many people formulate their concepts about the angelic realm from watching old TV productions such as *Touched by an Angel*. Programs like this lead people to conclusions about what angels do and how they interact with men day by day.

We learn from the Bible that there are different orders of angels (Colossians 1:16); however, in this particular section, we are introduced to one, who, in one sense, is not an angel, even though He is called the Angel of the Lord.

John 1:18 might be the determining factor in identifying the person who wrestled with Jacob, as it states that no man has seen God at any time; it is Jesus who reveals the Father to mankind.

The One we are introduced to in Genesis 32 is the preincarnate Christ. Here, we see Him meeting Jacob in the moment of his greatest need. Touched by an angel was the experience of Jacob in the most desperate moment, at the time of his most desperate need. Here, God met him through the very circumstances of his life, and he was forever changed.

What lessons can we learn from this account from the life of Jacob?

Providential Care

The first lesson we learn is God's providential care.

Jacob had just left the house of his father-in-law Laban. He had been toiling there many years, not as the head of the household but, rather, living under the authority of his father-in-law. It was in that circumstance that God spoke to him; and Jacob responded in faith, a step of faith that would bring him face-to-face with God Himself.

Stop and think about it like this: As you obey the voice of God and take His path down the roadway of life, even though you may face insurmountable circumstances, God will take care of you. In Jacob's life, we see the very providential care of God. From this, we learn that if we obey the voice of God, we need not fear because God will take care of us.

In the first verses of Genesis 32, we see the providential care of God: *"And Jacob went on his way and the angels of God met him."*

What an awesome concept! As you go on your way, as you obey the voice of God, God is providentially watching over your life. This is where God met Jacob. When Jacob saw the angels, he said, "This is God's host." (Genesis 32:2). He named that particular place Mahanaim, which means "a double camp." Here was more than one camp. There was the earthly camp of Jacob, and there was also the heavenly camp of God. Jacob learned that wherever he pitched his tent, God, with His heavenly host, would pitch His tent to take care of him.

Jacob was about to go through the land of his brother Esau. Esau wanted to take Jacob's life. Have you ever felt pursued? Have you ever felt your life was in danger? Have you ever felt you could not take another step but God was telling you to move on? Often you are fearful and doubting, but if you will obey the voice of God, He will give you His providential care. What a tremendous lesson! The very host of God encamped around Jacob! In one sense, Jacob had double vision: the vision of his earthly circumstances and the vision of heavenly care.

As each of us obeys the voice of God on the road of life, we will face what we might think are insurmountable circumstances. If we obey the voice of God, we can count on the providential care of God in ways we may not even know or see. The host of God encamped over Jacob, ready to take care of him at this moment of need. Are you in a moment of need? Do you need God's providential care? Rest assured, just as with Jacob, God will give you His providential care. Isn't it awesome to realize that God is always caring for us, even if we cannot see it with our human eyes?

The first lesson we can learn from Jacob's being touched by an angel, the Angel of Jehovah, the preincarnate Christ, is God's providential care.

Past Concerns

The second lesson we see is the past concerns. Jacob had an unresolved conflict with his brother Esau, and that conflict was a tremendous concern to him.

> "And the messengers returned to Jacob, saying, We came to thy brother Esau, and also he cometh to meet thee, and four hundred men with him. Then Jacob was greatly afraid and distressed: and he divided the people that was with him, and the flocks, and herds, and the camels, into two bands; and said, If Esau come to the one company, and smite it, then the other company which is left shall escape." (Genesis 32:6-8)

Past concerns—Jacob's relationship with Esau had developed into one of hatred, war, and danger. The Bible says he was distressed and greatly afraid. With fear and trepidation, he took each step. In his mind's eye, around the corner, behind the rocks, could be the end of part of his clan. His concerns heightened with the announcement that Esau was coming to meet him with four hundred soldiers. What fear and distress gripped his heart because of past concerns over unresolved conflict!

Do you feel threatened by past concerns in your own life—concerns that bring distress just by the memory, the thought, or just a word by someone? The fear and distress Jacob was experiencing was the result of forgetting about God's providential care.

Have you noticed that sometimes, even after the most wonderful and comforting times from the Word of God, past concerns come into your life. These concerns seem to erase the precious truths from your heart and mind and bring you back to a place where you are so distressed that you can hardly think about the promises of God's providential care. This is where we find Jacob. He had just experienced this tremendous encounter, where he saw beyond his earthly condition to the heavenly care God was providing. Yet with this announcement came such distress that he forgot all about God's care at least for the moment. What past concerns are robbing you of your present comfort? Remember, the host encamped over and around us is there to care for us.

The chorus, "Turn your eyes upon Jesus," reminds us of His providential care in the midsts of our past concerns.

Charles Haddon Spurgeon said, "We write our blessings in the sand and engrave our problems in stone."

So truly, my friend, we need to turn our eyes upon Jesus.

A Penitent Cry

A third lesson we see from the time when Jacob was touched by the Angel of the Lord is a penitent cry. Notice what Jacob says in Genesis 32:9-11:

> "And Jacob said, O God of my father Abraham, and God of my father Isaac, the LORD which saidst unto me, Return unto thy country, and to thy kindred, and I will deal well with thee: I am not worthy of the least of all the mercies, and of all the truth, which thou hast showed unto thy servant; for with my staff I passed over this Jordan; and now I am become two bands. Deliver me, I pray thee, from the hand of my brother, from the hand of Esau: for I fear him, lest he will come and smite me, and the mother with the children."

Jacob was so wrapped up in his past concerns, so distressed and fearful, but praise God, he looked up and said, "O God of my father Abraham, and God of my father Isaac." Then in this penitent cry, he made a marvelous declaration: "I am not worthy of the least of all thy mercies." Jacob started to see himself in the light of reality.

Have you ever thought like this? Sometimes God will allow fears of past concerns to grip your soul so you might fall on your knees and see yourself as God sees you. When you do, then you will cry out in humility, "I am not worthy of the least of all thy mercies."

This truth is also reflected in Paul's words to the Corinthians: "And the base things of the world, and the things which are despised, hath God chosen . . ." (1 Corinthians 1:28)

I have found in my own life that God may allow distresses to enter so I might see that the victory is not of myself but of God. These times help me understand how much I need God, and they help me cry out with this tremendous confession, "God, I am not worthy of the least of Thy mercies." When was the last time you did that? Or are you that one raising your head in pride and saying "God, I have done this or that. Therefore, you are obligated to do this or that for me"? No, it is not like that at all. You see, God chooses to use the weak to do wonderful things.

God uses the frail to carry out His fight. It is so important for you to come to the place where you cry out to God, not just from your lips but from your soul, saying "God, I'm not worthy."

Although he prayed for deliverance from his brother Esau, Jacob really needed deliverance from himself. The greatest deliverance you will experience, from the greatest enemy you have besides Satan himself, is deliverance from yourself. We all need to ask God, "Deliver me from myself."

"Jacob" means "schemer, trickster." He was the type who always had everything figured out. He arranged all the details so that everything would fall his way. He planned in minute detail, always scheming after the blessings of God. This is not God's way! God's way is a heart that cries out, "I am not worthy of the least of thy mercies," "Deliver me, not just from Esau but also from myself!"

In one sense, Esau represents the flesh. How we need daily deliverance from the flesh! Have you ever cried this penitent cry, "God, deliver me from myself"?

Pitiful Condition

The fourth lesson we see is derived from Jacob's pitiful condition. Here, we see the instability of Jacob, the schemer. After Jacob cried to God, it appears he went down again into the valley of despair. Jacob again looked out on his brother Esau, and he feared for his life. Notice what he said to his servants in Genesis 32:16-18:

> "And he delivered them into the hand of his servants, every drove by themselves; and said unto his servants, Pass over before me, and put a space betwixt drove and drove. And he commanded the foremost, saying, When Esau my brother meeteth thee, and asketh thee, saying, Whose art thou? and whither goest thou? and whose are these before thee? Then thou shalt say, They be thy

servant Jacob's; it is a present sent unto my lord Esau: and, behold, also he is behind us."

A pitiful condition—he is still scheming. He still tried to do it himself. Even after his tremendous penitent cry, he divided up the sheep, goats, and all his goods. Next, he told his servants to go before him and tell Esau that the animals were presents for him. Still scheming!

Stop and think about your own life. How many times, after you cry out to God, acknowledging Him as God, acknowledging your own unworthiness and crying out for his deliverance, do you go back to scheming? This is a pattern those like Jacob are prone to repeat. This can almost be seen as the threshold of transformation for Jacob. He still clung to his own plans, his own schemes, and hadn't let them go.

Can you just imagine what his servants thought? Didn't Jacob say we had a host of angels encamped around us? Didn't he say God was going to take care of us? Why the scheme? Why all the fretting? Why all the frustration? His lips say one thing; his life says something totally different.

Be aware, God will keep at you again and again until you let go of your plans, until you stop trying to operate through your power to accomplish your purposes. You need to learn to let go and let God do it.

Prevailing Combat

Next, we will see Jacob's prevailing combat. He went to war. He started to wrestle. This was a wrestling match that would leave a lasting mark on his life.

A man who was hurrying through life ended up hobbling through life, but he accomplished more through his hobbling than he ever did through his hurrying. Notice what the text says in Genesis 32:24: "And Jacob was left alone; and there wrestled a man with him until the breaking of the day."

The first step in this prevailing combat is that it was a private wrestling match. Often the greatest things God will do in your life will not be in public but in private. It's when you come to hand-to-hand combat with yourself, under the very wrestling match with the Lord Himself, that God does tremendous things in your life.

When was your last private encounter with God? When was the last time the Lord God of the universe reached down and you wrestled with God? It is a private issue. Those who do not have these private encounters have very hollow public experiences. Prevailing combat with God is a private matter.

Second, it's a personal matter. The text says again and again that Jacob wrestled with Him, the preincarnate Christ. He wrestled with Him. It's private. No one sees that but you and God. How much of your faith comes from your personal relationship with the Lord? Here, He appears as the Angel of the Lord, the preincarnate Christ. Some are born in Christian homes and know the words, prayers, and go through all the motions, but their faith never becomes personal. A prevailing combat with God is private, and it is personal.

Finally, it is passionate. The day was breaking, and the Lord has already touched the hollow of Jacob's thigh, causing it to go out of joint. Jacob desired to be set free, but notice what he said: "I will not let thee go except thou bless me."

That is pretty passionate. This is where the victory starts to come. "God, we are wrestling together in prayer, and I will not let you go until you bless me." Passionate!

Do you mean business with God? Are your prayers vain repetitions, or do they become passionate words of prevailing prayer? God, I am not going to let you go. You have already touched me, and I am hobbling around, but until I get your blessing on my life, I will not leave this place.

To this day, Jewish people do not eat certain parts of the legs of animals (the sciatic nerve and associated blood vessels and tendons) out of respect for Jacob's leg wound.

We can learn great lessons from this man who was touched by the angel. A man who was a schemer became a prince. "I will not let you go unless you bless me."

So God said, "All right, I am going to change your name. No longer will you be called Jacob, but now your name will be Israel. No longer a schemer, but now you will be called a prince, one who persists with God, who prevails with God." Through Jacob, a whole nation was blessed.

There are generations coming after you that will be blessed if you wait on God and persist in saying "God, I want your blessing in my life."

My prayer for you is that you would have an experience like this with God so that others would say, "He or she has been touched by God." Future generations will be blessed because of it.

Men who have touched my life have demonstrated the touch of God on their lives, and I am moved—"to go and do likewise."

As we come to a close to the jigsaw puzzle of life, maybe you are saying, "Joe, all I have is scattered and shattered pieces, and nothing fits in my life." My dear friend, the center piece that makes everything fit is the Lord Jesus Christ and His precious Word.

My first question for you is, do you know Him today as your personal Savior? If not, would you just trust Him right now as your Savior?

Just answer this question: Have you any room for Jesus?

An old Gospel song says it this way:

> Have you any room for Jesus,
> He who bore your load of sin?
> As He knocks and asks admission
> Sinner, will you let Him in?
> Room for Jesus, King of Glory
> Hasten now His Word obey;
> Swing the heart's door widely open,
> Bid Him enter while you may.

Maybe you know the Savior but are struggling to put the jigsaw puzzle of your life together. I will tell you, be it the pieces of what you believe or how you should behave as a child of God, the answers are found in God's instruction book for every piece of the jigsaw puzzle of life—the immutable, infallible, inspired Word of God.

I am reminded of the words of the psalmist: "Thou wilt show me the path of life: in thy presence is fullness of joy; at thy right hand there are pleasures for evermore."

So open the manual, pick up the pieces, and the Lord will work in and through you to not only to put together the jigsaw puzzle of life but also to help you rejoice in the pleasure of assembling a beautiful picture of His grace.

START TODAY IN THIS EXCITING ADVENTURE!

Endnotes

Chapter One

[1] Francis A. Schaeffer. He Is There and He Is Not Silent. Wheaton, IL: Tyndale House Publishers, 1981, p. 18.

Chapter Two

[1] Charles C. Ryrie. So Great Salvation, p. 93.

Chapter Four

[1] Dietrich Bonhoeffer. *Temptation*. New York, 1953, pp. 116-117.

Chapter Five

[1] Erwin Lutzer. *12 Myths That Americans Believe.* Chicago, IL: Moody Publication, 1993, p. 178.
[2] David Breese. Satan's Ten Most Believable Lies. Chicago, IL: Moody Publication, 1987, p. 8.

Chapter Six

[1] Kenneth A. Myers. *Christians and Popular Culture*, p. 18.
[2] R. C. Trench. *Synonyms of the New Testament*, p. 218.
[3] Max Lerner. *The Nation in the 1960s*, p. 225.

Chapter Seven

[1] Renald E. Showers. *The New Nature*, p. 155.

Chapter Nine

1. G. D. Watson (1845-1924), www.Bulletininserts.org.

Chapter Eleven

1. Dan Lucarini. *Why I Left the Contemporary Christian Music Movement* (Webster, NY: Evangelical Press, 2002), p. 94.
2. "Anything Goes: Taboos in the Twightlight," Newsweek, November 13, 1967, p. 75.
3. *Robert Jourdain, Music, the Brain, and Ecstasy* (New York, Avon books 1997) pp. 327-328.
4. Pastor Larry DeBruyn. *Drumming Up Deception* (Indianapolis, IN: Moeller Printing Company, Inc., 2008), p. 17.

Chapter Twelve

1. Laurie Cabot, "Power of the Witch," Masonic and Occult Symbols Illustrated by Dr. Cathy Burns, p. 301.

Chapter thirteen

1. Charles Bridges. Proverbs, The Banner of Truth, pp. 299-300.
2. Martin Lloyd Jones. "Christian Marriage: From Basic Principles to Transformed Relationships," *The Banner of Truth*.
3. Charles Bridges, *Proverbs, The Banner of Truth*, p. 300.
4. Ibid, p. 230.

Chapter fourteen

1. William Shakespeare. *Macbeth*, act 1, scene 3.
2. C. I. Scofield. *Prophecy Made Plain*, London, England: Pickering & Inglis, p. 14.
3. Charles L. Feinberg (editor). "Prophetic Truth Unfolding Today." E. Schuyler English. *The Church on Earth* (Westwood, NJ: Fleming H. Revell Company, 1968), p. 22.
4. Lewis Sperry Chafer. *Systematic Theology, Volume IV, Introduction to Eschatology* (Dallas, TX: Dallas Seminary Press, 1948), p. 257.
5. David Breese. *The Marks of a Cult* (Eugene, OR: Harvest House Publishers, 1998), p. 165.
6. Warren W. Wiersbe. *Be Real* (Wheaton, IL: Victor Books, 1979), p. 164.
7. Roy B. Zuck. "Balancing the Academic and the Spiritual in Seminary." Edited by Stanley D. Toussaint and Charles H. Dyer. *Essays in Honor of J. Dwight Pentecost* (Chicago, IL: Moody Press, 1986), p. 92.

[8] Benjamin Breckenridge Warfield. "Spiritual Culture in the Theological Seminary." *Princeton Theological Review*, January 1904, p. 70.

[9] Warren W. Wiersbe. *Real Worship* (Nashville, TN: Thomas Nelson Publishers, 1986), p. 81.

[10] Elizabeth Elliot, *The Journals of Jim Elliot* (Old Tappan, NJ: Fleming H. Revell Company, 1978), p. 18.

[11] John F. Walvoord, *The Revelation of Jesus Christ* (Chicago, IL: Moody Press, 1966), p. 273.

[12] Charles Caldwell Ryrie, *The Basis of the Premillennial Faith* (Neptune, NJ: Loizeaux Brothers, 1953), p. 15.

[13] Alfred p. Gibbs, *Worship, the Christian's Highest Occupation* (Kansas City, KS: Walterick Publishers, N. D), pp. 173-174.

[14] Author Unknown

[15] Wiersbe, *Real Worship*, p. 56.

[16] Scofield, *Prophesy Made Plain*, p. 19.

Chapter fifteen

[1] Poem by D. J. Higgins.

Chapter seventeen

[1] Walvoord. The Holy Spirit. Grand Rapids: Zondervan Publishing Co., 1954, p. 138.

[2] John F. Walvoord. *The Holy Spirit*. Grand Rapids: Zondervan Publishing Co., 1954, p. 155.

Printed in the United States
By Bookmasters